STRESS
MANAGEMENT
TECHNIQUES

STRESS MANAGEMENT TECHNIQUES

Managing People for Healthy Profits

Dr. Vernon Coleman

MERCURY

First published in 1988 by Mercury Books
Reprinted in paperback 1991
by Mercury Books
Gold Arrow Publications Ltd
London SW17 0NB

Set in Palatino by Input Typesetting Ltd, London
Printed and bound in Great Britain by
Mackays of Chatham PLC, Chatham, Kent

British Library Cataloguing in Publication Data

Coleman, Vernon
  Stress Management Techniques: Managing
  people for healthy profits
  1. Job stress   2. Personnel Management
  I. Title
  658.3'82   HF5548.85

  ISBN 1–85252–025–6

Stress costs your company £1,000 per employee per year.

If your company employs 1,000 people then stress costs the company £1,000,000 a year.

If your company employs 100 people then stress costs the company £400 a day.

In an average lifetime the average employee loses one and a half years from work because of stress-induced illness.

Whatever else you try, and however much you spend on high technology equipment, nothing will improve your company's efficiency and profitability more than taking care of your employees, reducing their exposure to stress and learning how to get the best out of them.

Your company's biggest hidden asset is the people it employs.

CONTENTS

Give people as much responsibility as they can
safely handle; Remember to say thank you;
Know when to push and when to stop; Smile
and the world will smile with you; Take the
terror out of computerisation; Don't
underestimate the peril of boredom; Teach
people to accept change; Avoid too much
administration; Teach employees to recognise
their own stress signs; Never give authority
without responsibility and never give
responsibility without authority; Treat people
as people — not tools; Teach people to say
no; Make sure that people have proper control
over the machinery they use: Help employees

CONTENTS

Part 1

STRESS — THE GREAT DESTROYER

1 WHY STRESS CAUSES ILLNESS AND COSTS YOU MONEY

THE EXISTENCE and importance of stress in industry was first recognised in America in 1956. A machine operator called James Carter cracked up while working on the General Motors production line in Detroit. Mr Carter had what is now commonly known as a nervous breakdown and he sued General Motors, claiming that the stresses of his job had contributed to his condition. It was an important lawsuit. Carter won — and from that day onwards most executives and all lawyers in American industry took the relationship between stress and industry very seriously indeed.

But despite James Carter's lawsuit, executives around the rest of the world have been slow to recognise the importance of stress in industry.

Indeed, in some ways it is difficult to blame company executives for failing to understand the importance of stress. Up until fairly recently most doctors regarded 'stress' as a trivial problem and laughed at any suggestion that there could be a link between problems in the mind and problems affecting the body.

Less than ten years ago I wrote a book called *Stress Control* in which I put forward the view that nearly all the common twentieth century diseases are caused or made worse by stress. I argued that stress was the greatest environmental hazard of our time, that it cost industry many millions of pounds every year and that doctors should be spending more time helping to prevent unnecessary stress, rather than simply treating symptoms.

At the time many doctors dismissed it all as hypo-thetical nonsense. Even some leading academic medical scientists still believed that all disease had a physical basis.

Today, I doubt very much if there is a doctor or repu-table medical scientist anywhere in the world who doesn't accept that stress (by that I mean anything that causes fear, anxiety, worry, apprehension, anger and even excitement) can cause quite genuine physical responses and very real diseases.

The figures vary from report to report but at a conserva-tive estimate at least three quarters of the illnesses treated by doctors are completely or largely psychosomatic in origin. If you include all the illnesses not seen by doctors — and that means such problems as backache, headaches, mild anxiety, sleeplessness, colds and so on — then the figures will be even more startling.

After talking to experts working in many different areas of medicine I would estimate that between 90% and 95% of all illnesses can be blamed totally or mainly on psycho-logical forces. Our minds are killing us and, as a side effect, ruining the economy.

Consider the common or garden headache. It is perfectly true that some headaches are caused by injuries and brain tumours but experts agree that at least 98 per cent of all headaches are stress and pressure related. When under stress we screw up our eyes and tighten and tense the muscles around our heads — and we get headaches.

Or take indigestion — one of the commonest disorders known to twentieth century man. It is so common that if five people sit down to dinner the chances are that after-wards at least one of them will have stomach pains. Occasionally, indigestion may be caused by poor eating habits or by eating the wrong sort of food. But in the vast majority of cases it is caused by anxiety.

Even when indigestion seems to be caused by bad

eating habits it is often easy to show the root cause to be stress. When a salesman hurries his lunch he is probably hurrying because he is under stress. When an office manager swallows food without chewing it is probably because she is desperate to get back to work and sort out problems that have accumulated. When a man grabs a sandwich while he works at his desk it is more than possible that he is feeling anxious about his work.

In the last few years evidence has accumulated from around the world to show that of the different types of stress that cause illness and disease the most common and most destructive is stress at work. Researchers have not only built up evidence showing links between industrial stresses in general and ill health but have even accumulated evidence showing that it is possible to link specific occupations with specific types of stress induced disease. No one is immune. The man or woman on the shop floor is just as vulnerable as the man or woman on the board. The man with virtually no responsibility may be just as vulnerable as the woman with an enormous amount. It is not just high-powered executives who suffer from stress induced disease.

Although there is absolutely no doubt that stress *is* killing many people, disabling many more and costing industry billions of pounds every year, there is one important question that has to be asked: *Why* are we so susceptible to stress these days?

Think about it carefully and you might imagine that we have good, stress-free lives.

Most of us get enough to eat, have somewhere warm and dry to sleep at night, don't have to worry too much about being eaten by wild animals and have the choice of several TV channels for our entertainment. We have central heating, motor cars, bank accounts and so many material goods that we don't know what to buy one another at Christmas time.

It would be easy enough to understand if our ancestors suffered a lot from stress. They had to worry about getting enough to eat, finding somewhere warm and dry to sleep at night and staying alive while marauding wild animals wandered around.

But compared to them we have it easy. You'd think that stress would be the last thing that would trouble us.

And yet stress is the twentieth century equivalent of the plague.

The answer to this apparently unanswerable paradox is quite simple.

Our bodies were designed a long, long time ago. We were not designed for the sort of world in which we live today. We were designed for a world in which fighting and running were useful practical solutions to everyday problems. We were designed to cope with physical confrontations with sabre–toothed tigers.

We are, I'm afraid, out of date.

The problem is that our environment has changed far more rapidly than we have evolved. We have changed our world far faster than our bodies have been able to adapt. At no other time in the history of the world has there been such a constant progression of ideas. Fashions, themes and attitudes have never changed as rapidly as they have in the last hundred years or so. Never before have expectations and pressures been so great. Revolutionary changes in agriculture, navigation, medicine, military tactics, design, transport, communications and industrial methods have all transformed our world. But our bodies are still the same as they were tens of thousands of years ago. It takes millenia for the human body to adapt. We have moved far too quickly for our own good.

Let me explain what I mean.

Imagine, for a moment, that you are a caveman. You and your mate live in a hole in the rock which you share with one other couple and a handful of assorted children. Your main problems every day are finding enough food to eat and getting hold of enough wood to keep your fire burning. You also have to avoid the local sabre–toothed tiger and occasionally you need to find yourself a new club or get your mate to make you a new loin cloth.

That's it. The pressures and problems you face are fundamental and straightforward. Your expectations are simple and easily defined.

Now, imagine an average sort of morning. You climb out from underneath a few old bear skins and you throw a few logs on the fire to take away the harsh morning chill. You look around the cave and see that you are right out of food. You need to catch something soon. So you pick up your spear, kiss your mate good-bye and set off into the jungle.

After half an hour or so you find yourself a nice, plump looking boar.

But at exactly the same moment as you spot the boar he spots you. Suspicious of your motives, he puts his head down and charges straight at you. You have five or six seconds to decide exactly what to do. If you make the right sequence of decisions then you'll have breakfast, lunch and dinner for the next few days. If you make the wrong decision you won't be worrying too much about breakfast or any other meals.

Within a few microseconds your body has responded to the threat in a very positive way. Your heart will have started to beat faster, your blood pressure will go up, your muscles will tense and acid will pour into your stomach. All these are sound and valuable physiological responses. And they help you to stay alive.

With more blood being pumped around your body and with your blood pressure rising you are more able to respond, to move quickly and effectively. With your muscles tense you are better equipped for fighting, running and climbing. And the acid pouring into your stomach ensures that any food still lying there is quickly turned into valuable energy.

The end result is that you move quickly and easily. You jump up into a nearby tree and, as the wild boar runs underneath you, reach down and club it to death. Your physical responses to a stressful situation have saved your life and enabled you to win a vital battle.

The crisis over, you slowly drag the beast back to your cave. As you do so your blood pressure gradually falls, your heart beat returns to normal and your muscles relax a little. The problem, a purely physical one, has been solved by a purely physical response. If you hadn't responded properly to that immediate stress you would probably have died. You would certainly have gone hungry.

Now come back to life at the end of the twentieth century. Think yourself through a fairly ordinary, routine day.

You wake up in your expensively decorated, centrally heated, comfortable bedroom. There are so many clothes hanging in your wardrobe that choosing what to wear takes several minutes. You refresh yourself in a shower of heated water. You enjoy a freshly cooked breakfast without any difficulty whatsoever.

Unlike your caveman ancestor you have no fundamental fears or unmet needs.

But there are problems.

Your daily newspaper carries a story suggesting that a major supplier of yours may be about to go bankrupt. There is news that the bank rate may rise. That will mean your mortgage rate will rise too. And a scare on the Japanese stock market means that unit trusts that you bought last month have crashed to three quarters of their previous value.

In the mail there are a number of unpleasant letters. There is a hefty telephone bill — showing three transatlantic calls that you can't remember making — a bill for school fees and a bill from the garage. There is an invitation to a party at the Henrys' (you can't stand them but daren't refuse the invitation because Norman Henry is President of the local golf club and you're desperately anxious to join), and a letter from your mother asking why you haven't been to see her for such a long time.

As you struggle through the daily newspaper and the mail you hurry your breakfast. Eating too quickly gives you indigestion. You take a couple of antacid tablets. What a fine start to the day.

When you get into the car you discover it is almost out of petrol. You meant to fill it up last night but you were in such a hurry that you didn't have time. The tape player doesn't work and that funny 'knocking' noise just over the back axle is back again.

The main route to your office is jammed solid with cars and lorries. The local council is doing roadworks and the holdups seem to have been going on for ever. Trying to catch up on lost time you ambitiously attempt to move between a slow moving Morris Minor and a milk float. The result is a nasty scratch all down one side of your car.

And a broken wing mirror.

At the office you discover that your secretary is away ill. She has another of her migraines. That is the fourth time this month and you are really going to have to think about replacing her with someone more reliable. There is a memo from the European Marketing Director asking to see you urgently (he has a number of problems with an exhibition the company is trying to mount in Frankfurt) and a series of urgent messages from the Chairman's office. Rumour of a potential takeover bid has apparently been substantiated and the Chairman wants your view. An urgent board meeting is being convened for the after-noon. It looks likely to go on for half the night.

And just as you prepare yourself for a long day you get a phone call from home reminding you that you're supposed to be entertaining friends to dinner and asking you to pick up a red pepper and two kilos of roasted peanuts.

And so it goes on. Every minute of every hour is filled with problems, anxieties, worries, fears and crises. None of them threatens your life but all are important: they all threaten your *way of life*. They all threaten YOU.

As a result your body responds to each of these threats in a powerful, physical way. When you open your newspaper and find that the base lending rate has gone up your blood pressure rises, your heart beats faster, your muscles tense and acid pours into your stomach. When you open the mail and find a hefty telephone bill in front of you your heart beats faster, your blood pressure goes up, acid pours into your stomach and your muscles become tense. When you find yourself stuck in a traffic jam, knowing that you are going to be late, your muscles tense, acid pours into your stomach, your blood pressure goes up and your heart beats faster. When you arrive at work and find that there are problems in Frankfurt, acid pours into your stomach, your blood pressure goes up, your muscles tense and your heart beats faster.

You respond to every problem in the same way that your ancestor responded to the wild boar rushing straight at him. Your body responds to all those threats in the only way it knows how: it assumes that a straightforward physical response will improve your chances of survival.

Your physical response is outdated and inappropriate. Your body responds in that way because your body has not been able to evolve fast enough to cope with life in the twentieth century. The world around has changed dramatically in the last few centuries but your body still responds in a simple, crude way.

In the last few score years we have invented the office, the car, the telephone, the typewriter and the computer. We have altered our world so much that we are no longer able to live in it comfortably.

The result is that by the end of the day your blood pressure has reached a dangerously high level; your muscles are so tense that you have a headache and a pain in your back; your heart is beating far too quickly and your stomach is half eaten away by the amount of acid that has been produced.

STRESS – THE GREAT DESTROYER

None of this would matter too much if tomorrow was going to be any different. But it isn't. Tomorrow there will be more worries.

There will be worries about the visitors you are expecting at the weekend, the washing machine that has broken down, the skiing holiday that the children are expecting, the fault that has developed in the microwave oven, the problem in your New York office, the continued absence of your secretary, the industrial dispute that has developed at your factory in Liverpool and the rising price of copper tubing.

And to each and every one of your problems your body will respond in a positive and potentially dramatic way.

Is it any surprise that by the time he is 40 years old the average British employee in an average sort of job has high blood pressure, an early peptic ulcer, recurrent backache and difficulty in sleeping? Is it any surprise that in any large company there will be scores of employees who are clinging to sanity and good health by their finger nails and for whom a cruel word or a minor insult may trigger a major personal disaster?

You don't have to be a well paid executive in a position of responsibility to suffer in this sort of way. These days every single one of us is exposed to pressure and stress and every single one of us responds in the same simple, outdated, damaging sort of way.

The problems may vary but the responses do not.

So, for example, the man who has a job on the factory floor worries about the new machinery that is being installed. Will it make him redundant? He worries about the payments on his car. Will he still be able to afford them when interest rates rise? He worries about the rumour that the company he works for is about to be taken over. Will it mean that the factory will close? He worries about the row that he had with the foreman. And he worries about the size of his gas bill.

The President of the Company worries too. He worries

about the threatened takeover bid because he suspects that if the company loses the battle his job will go. He worries about his wife's drinking problem. He worries about having to make a speech at a trade dinner. He worries about the forthcoming shareholders' meeting. He worries about the latest figures from the company's subsidiary in Brazil. He worries about the price of sterling. He worries about the cost of having his pool repaired. And he worries about his mistress who has threatened to tell all if he doesn't leave his wife and move in with her.

Stress. It is around us all the time. None of us is immune to the damage it does.

According to recently published research more than 6 out of every 10 employees in the United Kingdom feel that their lives are 'significantly stressed'. The research showed that more than 7 out of every 10 stressed employees said they felt edgy and bad tempered; more than 5 out of every 10 had difficulty in making decisions and in concentrating; and 6 out of 10 said that they found it difficult to relax. Just under 4 out of every 10 confessed that stress was ruining their love lives.

2 HOW STRESS DOES THE DAMAGE

STRESS HAS an effect on industrial efficiency and corporate profits in a number of quite specific ways. These effects are, of course, all closely interlinked.

First, and perhaps most obviously, there is the effect that stress has on the individual's health. I honestly doubt if there is a single illness known to man (or woman) that is not now recognised as being either directly caused or indirectly exacerbated by stress.

There may be other causative factors of course. But whether the problem be alcoholism, angina, arthritis or asthma, there is no doubt that pressure and anxiety can always make things worse.

With this link in mind look now at the amount of money your company loses through sickness. Figures vary from industry to industry and from company to company but you may well find that between 5 and 10 per cent of your annual wages bill is paid to people who aren't working but who are at home, in hospital or convalescing. In some industries the sickness rate is considerably higher than this.

(Oddly enough, you will probably also find that most of your company's employees will, over a long period of time, lose much the same sort of total time through sickness. Some workers will lose their sick time in odd days taken here and there while others will go for years without losing any time at all and will then need six months off work because of a heart attack or stroke.)

I am not, of course, suggesting that all the time lost

through sickness is a direct result of stress. But I can assure you that there is overwhelming evidence to show that *most* of this lost time is a direct result of stress.

Some illnesses are more closely linked to stress than others. For example, at least three quarters of the working days lost through indigestion, backache and anxiety are directly stress related. Stress plays a vital part in determining the amount of time needed off work by patients suffering from heart disease, pre-menstrual tension, menopausal problems and high blood pressure. Peptic ulceration is invariably caused or made worse by stress. Skin diseases such as eczema and dermatitis are stress related. Migraine, insomnia, colds and flu, overeating, colitis and memory lapses are all problems known to be usually caused by stress.

Stress is the twentieth century plague. We have succeeded in conquering most of the infectious diseases that caused such havoc in the nineteenth century. Smallpox, typhoid, cholera and tuberculosis are little more than memories. Today stress is the big killer.

Find out what your company pays out to employees who are off work sick. *At least* half that sum is the basic price your company is paying for doing too little to combat the twentieth-century plague.

The ultimate consequence of stress induced illness is a stress induced death. Again, there is evidence to show that the number of people dying from diseases caused by stress is also on the increase. Look through your company payroll and find out how many employees have died of heart disease, strokes and cancer while in their thirties, forties and fifties. Every single one of those deaths is a tragedy. But most of those deaths were stress induced and avoidable.

Just in case you have difficulty in converting sadness and sympathy into figures that the company's accountants will understand, let me also point out that the people most likely to die at an early age are the very people whom the company can least afford to lose: the hard working men and women who have taken upon themselves the major burdens of industrial life.

According to figures taken directly from the British Registrar General's Occupational Mortality tables, company directors are seven times as likely as clerical workers to have a heart attack; five times as likely to develop duodenal ulcers; seven times as likely to commit suicide and nearly twenty times as likely to have a stroke.

The people who are most likely to die young are the people who have allowed themselves to carry the greatest burden. They pay for their dedication with their lives. The company pays by losing its most loyal and hard working employees.

Sickness and death are two of the most dramatic ways that stress can cost a company money. But they are not by any means the only ways in which stress can damage the company balance sheet.

Unhappiness, frustration, boredom and too much responsibility are all common causes of stress that can lead to poor productivity, lost sales and a general lack of interest in the company's future. Workers under these types of stress are likely to take time off on Friday afternoons and Monday mornings; they are likely to take off a few days every year for some undisclosed personal 'illness'.

Perhaps most important of all, workers who are stressed by their jobs are likely to be inefficient and incompetent.

The telephone operator who doesn't care will take an inordinate amount of time to answer an outside telephone call — and the company may lose an important order. The salesman who is under too much stress will visit his next client with a gloomy look on his face and a sag in his shoulders. He won't get any orders. The stores foreman who feels aggrieved will pilfer. The accountant who can't cope with the pressure will drink too much and make appalling mistakes.

And, of course, workers who are unhappy or who are

under too much stress are quite likely to leave and look for work elsewhere. In some industries job 'hopping' is commonplace and is accepted as inevitable by managements who do not understand what it means when people are desperate to leave their work.

I am frequently told that in the retail trade a high staff turnover is acceptable as inevitable. That is simply not true. With thought and care the turnover of staff could be dramatically cut. When you consider the amount of money that has to be spent on advertising for new employees, training them and providing them with uniforms etc. then you begin to realise just how expensive this aspect of stress can be.

All this is merely the visible tip of a very large, very damaging iceberg. The loss in terms of performance impaired by stress is incalculable. A man or woman under stress is prone to make mistakes. Many errors in management, on the factory floor and in the office can be blamed on stress.

But just spend a few moments with a calculator looking at the specific areas I have outlined and you'll soon see the phenomenal cost of stress to your company.

3 HOW OUR MINDS ARE KILLING OUR BODIES

THERE ARE many strange things about stress but the oddest is the fact that there doesn't seem to be any simple, straightforward correlation between the existence of stress and the development of stress induced disease. Some individuals seem to suffer enormously when under quite modest amounts of stress while others are able to cope with enormous amounts. There are, indeed, many people who actually seem to thrive on stress.

Let me give you a few examples.

George Huntingdon is the sales director of a fairly large publishing company. I've known him for some years now and if there is one word that sums up George it is that he is a 'worrier'. He is full of anxieties. When his company introduces its autumn book list he worries incessantly that the editorial people may have picked all the wrong books. When a book sells particularly well he worries about whether or not the printers and binders are going to be able to produce enough books to meet the demand.

When the weather is good he worries in case bookshop customers all decide to go sunbathing. When the weather is bad he worries in case all the potential customers stay at home by their firesides. When there is a fall in the value of the pound he worries about the cost of buying books from America. When there is a rise in the value of the pound he worries about the difficulties the company will have when trying to sell books abroad.

In theory George really doesn't have too many worries. His father founded the company for which he works. He himself owns quite a large amount of stock in the company. He owns a large house in Hampstead that must be worth half a million pounds at the very least. He has a beautiful, loyal wife, two small healthy children, a new BMW and a cottage in Gloucestershire.

But in practice George reacts badly to every ounce of stress and every imagined disaster. He is a walking dictionary of stress induced disease. He suffers from persistent and unsightly eczema on his hands. He suffers from asthma and his blood pressure is slightly raised. He isn't yet 40 years old but he has already been turned down by two life insurance companies. He only managed to get a policy on his life by paying a very hefty premium.

At the other end of the stress spectrum there is Micky Nicholson. I've known Micky for ten years now and he is a phenomenon. He has always been a bit of a wheeler dealer and I don't think I know anyone who sails quite as close to the wind as he does. For the last five years he has been building up a computer company. He knows absolutely nothing about computers and yet he has made himself a millionaire several times over.

Micky has succeeded by taking chances. About eighteen months ago he confessed to me that after his computer company had been in business for two years he had four different bank loans to service. Every month he had to find over thirty thousand pounds just to pay the interest. At the time, his assets were negligible. The only thing he actually owned was a wardrobe full of expensive suits.

You'd imagine that someone who takes as many chances would be a nervous wreck. There can't be many people who've put themselves under as much stress as Micky has.

But he's one of the healthiest people I know. In the ten years I've known him he's needed treatment only for two sexually transmitted diseases and a verruca that he swears he picked up at his squash club. He hasn't lost a day's work or a night's sleep.

The reason for these apparent anomalies is that stress

itself never causes any problems at all. It is not the existence of stress that causes damage so much as the way we
respond to that stress. It is not the changes or the pressures that produce the anxiety or the heart disease but
the individual's inability to cope with the difficulties and
strains produced by those changes.

Each one of us has two fairly fixed stress thresholds.
At one end of the spectrum we can all cope with only so
much activity (the amount, of course, varies from one
individual to another). At the other end of the spectrum
we can only cope with so much inactivity. If you are a
person with a low stress threshold for activity then you
are likely to respond badly when you are under pressure.
If you have a low stress threshold for inactivity then you
will respond badly when you haven't got enough to keep
you busy. Boredom will be your downfall. If the range
between your two stress thresholds is narrow then you
will be particularly likely to suffer from stress. If the range
between your two thresholds is wide then you are likely
to suffer relatively little from stress.

Stress is the root cause of most twentieth century
diseases — and responsible for billions of pounds worth
of losses every year in industry — but stress itself never
kills or harms anyone. Stress doesn't cost your company
a penny. It is the way that people respond to stress that
does the damage.

It is also important to remember that most twentieth
century pressures are abstract, not real. It is not what is
really happening around us that produces a reaction: it is
what we suspect might be happening, it is what we think
is likely to happen, it is what we imagine. The damage
that is done by twentieth century stress is done through
our minds.

Take Brian, for example. He works for a large car
component manufacturer and has a well paid job with
them. He is married and has one son of nineteen studying
to be a teacher. When I first saw Brian he was lying in
bed recovering from a heart attack. He readily confessed

that he felt sure his heart attack had been brought on by the pressure he'd been under. He said that nearly all this pressure was related to his job. When I asked him to explain to me exactly what sort of stresses he had to cope with he thought for a long moment before answering.

'It's difficult to say,' he confessed. 'There are so many different pressures that it's hard to know where to start. But to give you an idea,' he went on, 'one of my most important functions is to buy in raw materials. If I don't get the raw materials to the factory on time then we can't make our products. That is worrying.'

'*Why* is it worrying?' I asked him.

He looked puzzled.

'I know it's your job to get the materials to the factory,' I explained. 'But exactly *why* do you worry if it looks as if there is going to be a shortage?'

Brian looked uncomfortable.

'Is it because you don't do your job particularly well?' I asked him.

'No, it's certainly not that,' said Brian. 'I'm very conscientious and I've always done my best for the firm. It's just that sometimes things happen that are outside my control.'

'So, why do you worry?'

'Well, I suppose because I think that if anything goes wrong then my job will be on the line,' said Brian at last.

'Do you mean that you'd get the sack if a supplier didn't provide what you'd ordered?'

'Well, no, I don't suppose I'd get the sack,' admitted Brian.

'And what if you *did* get the sack?' I asked him. 'How terrible would that be?'

'Awful,' said Brian quickly. 'At my age I'd never get another job. I'd be on the scrap heap.'

'Is there anything you'd like to do but don't have the time to do?' I asked him.

'Lots of things,' he said. 'I write articles on angling for

a magazine. I'd like to turn them into a book one day if I had the time.'

'So you would have things to do if you lost your job?'

'Oh, yes,' Brian agreed. 'I'd have things to do. But I wouldn't have any money. Our house costs a lot to run you know.'

'How many bedrooms has your house got?' I asked.

Brian looked puzzled. 'Four,' he told me.

'How many do you need?' I asked. 'Really need?'

'One,' said Brian, after a moment or two. 'Two, perhaps, at most.'

'When did you buy your house?'

'Twenty years ago.'

'And it's probably worth a lot more than you paid for it?'

Brian nodded and smiled. 'It's worth quite a lot,' he admitted. 'People always say that it's wise to put your money into property and it's true.'

'So, if you sold it you could buy somewhere smaller and still be quite well off? Your outgoings would be reduced dramatically and you'd have some loose cash left over from the exchange of houses.'

Brian thought for a moment and then nodded. 'Yes, I suppose so,' he agreed.

'So getting the sack wouldn't be quite so terrible,' I said. 'You could buy somewhere smaller, enjoy life more and write your book on fishing.'

There was silence for a moment. 'I'd never thought of it like that before,' said Brian. 'Do you think that's what I should do?'

'No,' I said quickly, with a laugh. I explained that all I'd been trying to do was to point out that the stress that had probably caused his heart attack was largely in his mind — and largely based on false thoughts.

'Its been the way that you've thought about your work that has turned daily problems into health damaging stress,' I explained.

*

The fears that had run through Brian's daily thoughts didn't just make him ill. They would, almost certainly, also have damaged his ability to work effectively. A man who is forever worrying about his future will not work well. Too much of his mental effort will be wasted.

And Brian is by no means unusual, of course. In just about every company there are huge numbers of employees who respond not to the real pressures that surround them but to the pressures that they think are there. The stress that is killing your staff exists not in the real world but in the world that exists in their heads. There is plenty of natural stress in our lives but most of us make more stress for ourselves than we really need to suffer.

It isn't rising interest rates or low quality control or incompetent suppliers that cause ill health and lost working time; it is the way we respond to rising interest rates, low quality control and incompetent suppliers. And although many of the problems we fear *are* real, we do frequently create new fears and stresses out of thin air. Many of the pressures which kill are abstract and ethereal.

Sabre–toothed tigers can kill you with their claws or teeth. New rates demands and commercial disasters can kill you by the effect they have on your mind.

Each month something like six thousand medical journals are published around the world. A growing number of them are carrying reports of new evidence to illustrate the existence and importance of the vital link between mental pressure and physical and mental disease.

As far back as 1946 a research project started at Johns Hopkins University School of Medicine in Baltimore, involving nearly 1,500 medical students, was designed to investigate the relationship between attitudes and illness. The research programme lasted for seventeen years and suggested that the way an individual responds to pressure has powerful effects on the types of illnesses his body develops.

Since then an overwhelming amount of evidence has been produced to show the truth of that assertion. At a conference hosted by the Department of Epidemiology and Rheumatology at McMaster University in Ontario, Canada, there was near unanimous agreement that a patient's attitudes towards life directly affect both his physical and mental health. It has even been shown that when people fall ill their worries about their illness are likely to produce yet further problems and delay the rate at which they get better. The link between the mind and the body can produce a constricting, destructive circle of endless physical and mental distress.

This relationship between the mind and the body is so close that, even when a disease or an injury seems to have been caused by some entirely external force, the attitude of the individual concerned can have a powerful effect on the speed with which the damaged parts of the body recover. If you fall down and break your leg, the rate at which your broken bones mend will depend upon your attitudes, hopes, fears and aspirations.

The power of the mind over the body can even affect an individual's will to live and his chances of staying alive. Most of us in the Western world think of voodoo as something of a joke. We think it slightly bizarre that there are still people who can be so terrified by a threat uttered by a witch doctor that they will drop down dead within hours of being told that they will die.

And yet we are no different. It is just that our witch doctors, instead of wearing war paint, grass skirts and hideous masks, tend to wear dark trousers and white coats and have stethoscopes hanging round their necks. When a doctor tells a patient that he has just three months or six months to live then the chances are that the forecast will prove accurate and the patient will die on time. This isn't because doctors are particularly good at forecasting the life expectancy of their patients: it is because the power of the mind is so great that, often, when we are told we are going to die, we die.

*

[37]

Since it became clear that the mind does have power over the body, scientists have worked hard to try to show precisely how the functioning of the body can be influenced by transient thought processes. They have shown that it is through the medium of the imagination that the mind exerts much of its power. Our bodies are affected by what we think has happened, is happening or is likely to happen.

If you believe that you are going to be fired from your job, your body will respond in as dramatic a way as if you had been fired from your job.

In recent years scientists have even shown the power of the imagination to be so complete that apparently involuntary reflexes can be controlled by thought processes. For example, it seems that the body's automatic digestive processes can be controlled by the imagination.

In an experiment conducted a year or two ago volunteers were able to produce enzymes which their bodies did not need. Normally, if human beings eat meals that contain a good deal of fat, their bodies produce special enzymes which break down the fat and turn it into products easily transported in the blood. These enzymes are produced without any thought, and their production is controlled by a sophisticated series of internal reflexes.

Under experimental conditions, however, it was shown that if volunteers were told they had eaten fat when they hadn't, their bodies would respond to the imagined event rather than the truth. The fat dissolving enzymes were produced even though they weren't really needed.

In another experiment it was shown that the body's immune system can be controlled by using the imagination too. Normally, when human beings are given an intradermal tuberculin injection to find out whether they are immune to TB their bodies respond automatically. If the individual has been previously exposed to tuberculosis and has prepared internal immune defence systems, a swelling and a small red mark will develop at the site. If the individual has not previously been exposed to TB and has not developed any immune defences, no mark and no swelling will develop. This test is done routinely to find out whether patients need vaccinations.

Yet researchers have shown that the body's apparently entirely involuntary response to the testing injection can be regulated by the imagination. Some individuals who would normally have reacted to an intradermal injection of tuberculin do not do so, if told not to. The swelling and the red mark do not develop. The imagination can, it seems, even control a cell–mediated immunity reaction.

If the imagination can have such a powerful effect, its strength as a healing power must surely match its damaging potential. The most remarkable thing about the imagination is perhaps the way that we have been aware of its power without really recognising the importance of that power. It really isn't difficult to think of plenty of other examples of ways in which the imagination rules the body.

If you put a wooden plank on the floor and try to walk along it, you'll find it a remarkably easy task. Now, try telling yourself that the plank is suspended fifty feet above the floor, and that there are crocodiles waiting underneath for you to fall. The plank won't have altered in width or height above the floor. But you'll find walking along it a much more difficult task.

Football managers also know the value of the human imagination. If a player's mind tells him that he is tired, he will be tired. And he will find it difficult to keep running in the second half of the game. If all the players in a team believe they are going to lose, they will probably lose. If all the players in a team believe that they are going to win, they will probably win. The half time pep talk can make a staggering amount of difference to a team's success. The team manager or captain who can instil a sense of confidence and quiet determination in his team will be well worth his place for his qualities of leadership alone. Remember England cricket captain Mike Brearley?

Film directors have for years exploited the power of the

human imagination without really being fully aware of the power they have at their disposal. When a cinema patron settles down in his seat to enjoy a good film he will be lost in the fantasy world created for him. If the film is a good one, each member of the audience will forget he is sitting in a darkened room with several hundred other people. He won't hear the rustling of toffee papers or the crackle of popcorn. The illusion created on the screen will enable him to escape from the real world in which his body is imprisoned. His mind will wander freely, directed by the actions of the figures on the screen. And what is happening in his mind will rule what happens to his body too.

When the film Lawrence of Arabia was shown on the cinema screen, reports from around the world indicated that the sale of ice cream in those cinemas had rocketed. The endless desert scenes made the patrons feel uncomfortably hot. Their bodies responded to what they thought they were experiencing and during the intervals thousands of people bought themselves cooling ice creams.

You can even obtain much the same sort of genuine physical response by reading a good book. If the story is frightening you'll feel your pulse racing and the hairs standing up on the back of your neck. If the story is sad then the tears will start to pour down your cheeks. Your body will have responded to your imagination.

Another factor which has a powerful influence on the way an individual responds to stressful situations is the nature of his personality. There is now not only evidence to show that personality can have a tremendous influence on the way that someone's body responds to stress but to show that his personality influences the type of illness he subsequently develops.

Some of the research evidence linking personality type to specific types of disease is very old. In 1910 William Osler wrote in *The Lancet* that it was ambitious, hard working men who were the most likely to develop heart trouble. And in 1945 it was suggested that people who have heart attacks are often tortured by their need to compete with their fathers.

Since then a growing number of researchers have managed to amplify both these statements. In the 1950s Drs Rosenman and Friedman showed that the people who are most likely to get heart attacks are usually male and usually under a great deal of pressure. These patients with 'heart attack personalities' invariably have a strong drive to compete and to achieve. The heart attack patient, it seems, works long hours, sets out to succeed, finds it difficult to sit still, is unable to relax and is a perfectionist. No matter how successful he is, he will rarely be able to fully satisfy his ambitions. (And, of course, it's not how successful you are that determines your sense of personal satisfaction — its how successful you think you are.)

The evidence linking personality to cancer also goes back a long way. In the second century AD the Roman physician Galen noticed that women who were depressed were far more likely to develop cancer than women who were happy.

In recent years we've acquired a considerable amount of evidence to support that early observation. Today it is known that people who are cancer prone tend to try too hard to please the world. When they fail, as they invariably must (it is never possible to please all the people all of the time), they are more likely to develop cancer.

There is evidence showing that it is possible to link specific personality types to all sorts of diseases — arthritis, asthma, colitis, eczema, hay fever and migraine, for example. And there is even evidence to show that there are personality factors which determine who is most likely to suffer from colds and minor throat infections. It seems that the severity of the symptoms endured by someone who has a cold depends upon the amount of stress and strain that he thinks he is under.

Our personalities play a vitally important role in our lives. They determine the sort of immediate environment we create for ourselves and they then determine the way in which we respond to the stresses and strains that are inherent in that self–made environment. It is our minds which commonly kill our bodies. But it is our personalities which decide just how the killing is done.

Part 2

PEOPLE UNDER
PRESSURE

4 THE SIGNS AND SYMPTOMS OF STRESS

THERE ARE literally thousands of different signs and symptoms that show when people are under too much stress.

There are the embarrassing silences when someone more senior walks into an office; there are the flashes of unexpected aggression; the inexplicably ferocious industrial disputes; the unexpected arguments over holidays; the sudden increase in staff turnover; the increase in the amount of time being lost through sickness; the increase in the number of odd days lost through unexplained absenteeism; the pilfering. (Pilfering often occurs not necessarily because people want the stuff they are stealing but because they are angry, bored and frustrated, and desperate to strike back in some way.)

There are many more physical and mental symptoms.

Below I have listed just a few of the commoner symptoms that show when someone is under too much stress.

1. *An apparent change in personality or behaviour.* The individual who is under too much pressure may become irritable or aggressive. He may suddenly start to suffer from unaccountable and atypical memory lapses. He may start to stutter. He may develop strange and inexplicable obsessions, becoming an overdemanding perfectionist. He may suddenly burst into tears for no apparent reason or he may suddenly become silent and brooding. Alternatively, he may fly into a rage. Old friendships may be broken; emotions will not be explained or easily shared. Comments may be made which seem cruel and malicious.

If any of these symptoms do develop then think carefully about whether the symptoms could be due to too much stress. Think whether you could help by reducing the individual's exposure to pressure in some way.

2. *Workaholism.* The average workaholic finds it difficult to relax or take a holiday. He will spend evenings and weekends working and will constantly worry about what is going on at work. He will be the last one out at night and will turn up for work on bank holidays. When away from his office he will telephone in three times a day. He will have difficulty in sleeping and may wake up at night to carry on working.

He won't eat properly and will inevitably lose weight. His family life, hobbies and friendships will all suffer. He'll be edgy and restless when he isn't working and his physical and mental health will deteriorate. He will have an increased risk of developing a heart attack, peptic ulceration, high blood pressure or any one of the other problems known to be associated with heavy pressure and stress. He will have an increased risk of developing depression or some other serious mental problem.

Many people are pushed by regular stresses into an addiction to a workaholic lifestyle. They get hooked on the adrenalin 'kick' that they get from working. In the short term the workaholic can be a great asset to a company. But he has little long term value and really needs advice and support at an early stage.

3. *Signs of physical and mental illness.* People always tend to have a 'weak spot' which flares up when they are under too much stress. It is an early warning sign of distress. Learn to know what you're looking for and you can 'read' the people you work with as well as any physician — better, probably, since you have the advantage of knowing them better. Indigestion, wheezing attacks, diarrhoea and headaches are among the commonest physical symptoms that show that an individual has reached, and passed, his stress threshold.

The conditions most commonly associated with stress are:

accident proneness
addiction
alcoholism
allergic dermatitis
allergic rhinitis
alopecia
anaemia
angina pectoris
ankylosing spondylitis
anorexia
anxiety
aphthous ulcers
apoplexy
appetite loss
arrhythmia
arteriosclerosis
arthritis
asthma

backache
baldness
bedwetting
blood pressure
breathlessness
bronchitis

cancer
cardiac failure
cerebral arteriosclerosis

cerebral haemorrhage
cerebral thrombosis
cholecystitis
cold, common
colitis
constipation
cystitis

depression
dermatitis
diabetes
diarrhoea
digestive disorders
dizziness
duodenal ulcer
dysmenorrhoea (painful
   periods)
dyspepsia (indigestion)
dysphagia (difficulty in
   swallowing)

eczema
eneuresis (incontinence, bed
   wetting)
epilepsy

fainting
fear
flatulence

frigidity

gall bladder disease
gall stones
gastritis
gastroenteritis
giddiness
gout

habituation (of drugs)
hair loss
hay fever
headaches
heart attack
heart block
heart failure
heartburn
hepatitis
hypertension
hypochondriasis
hysteria

impotence
incontinence
indigestion
infarction
infective diseases
influenza
insomnia
intermittent claudication
irritability
ischaemic heart disease
itching

joint diseases

libido loss
lumbago

marriage problems
memory failure
menopausal problems
menstrual problems
migraine
myocardial infarction
myxoedema

nausea
nervous breakdown
nightmares

obesity
obsessions
osteoarthritis

palpitations
peptic ulceration
personality disorders
phobias
post baby blues
premenstrual tension
psoriasis
puerperal depression

reactive depression
rheumatism

sciatica

sexual problems	tumours
sickness	thyroid trouble
sleeplessness	thyrotoxicosis
stammer	
stroke	ulcers
stuttering	ulcerative colitis
suicide	
	vomiting
tension	
tremors	wheezing

Note that some of the disorders have other causes apart from stress. But stress is a common contributory cause and often exacerbates the symptoms that are produced.

4. *Watch the way that people walk and move and sit.* The individual who is under an enormous amount of stress may walk with his shoulders hunched and his head and neck held slightly forwards. His jaw may be clenched tightly, his voice may disappear from time to time, his breathing may be shallow and rather difficult. His hands may be held tightly clenched, his nails may be bitten and when he sits he will probably cross his legs, keeping the leg of the upper foot angled upright and bouncing up and down rhythmically. He may play with a ring on one of his fingers. He will probably fiddle with pencils and paperclips whenever he gets the chance — but he won't be content with fiddling: pencils may be broken and paper clips bent beyond recognition. His eyes may be fixed, staring into the distance. He may handle work like a robot, refusing eye contact with others and showing an unusual lack of interest in his work.

5. *Drug addiction* of one sort of another is probably one of the commonest consequences of stress. Occasionally, there are executives who get hooked on so called 'hard' drugs such as cocaine and heroin but addiction to commoner more readily available 'legal' drugs such as alcohol, tobacco and tranquillisers is much more common and, surprisingly perhaps, far more damaging.

Consider alcohol, for example.

Today alcohol is more easily produced and more widely available than a great many other substances whose effect on mood, perception, or behaviour are regarded with fear and suspicion. Indeed, all the evidence suggests that the production and consumption of alcohol is increasing at a tremendous rate. These days countries are losing their individual drinking patterns; everyone, women and teen-agers included, is using alcohol.

It is the effect alcohol has on the brain that makes it particularly attractive to individuals under stress. And it is the effect that alcohol has on the brain that makes it especially dangerous. Alcohol is detectable in the brain within half a minute of a glass being emptied. Once alcohol gets to the brain its first effect is depressant. If you drink a small amount the depressant effect seems to work most noticeably on the part of the brain that controls your tendency to get excited. With the controls depressed you become more talkative and more excitable. That is why we commonly consider alcohol to be a social lubri-cant. Social and personal inhibitions are lifted by alcohol and most people become much looser and less restricted by social convention when they have had a drink or two.

However, at the same time as alcohol is depressing inhibitions it also has other effects. The brain's ability to concentrate on information, understand messages that it is receiving and make judgements on those messages will diminish. Reflexes will go and, although the individual won't be aware of it, his ability to link sensory input to muscular function will be badly distorted. The person who has been drinking will think that he will be able to talk, dance, negotiate or drive a car more efficiently than normal whereas in fact his ability to do these things will be adversely affected. The businessman who drinks too much during or before a meeting will probably make bad decisions and offer poor advice to those who are dependent upon his expert opinion.

The major risk for a drinker is, of course, that he will become an alcoholic. According to the World Health Organization between 1 and 10 per cent of the world's population can now be properly described as alcoholics. Something like one in every three drinkers is already in this category or is heading for it. Once someone has become an alcoholic then he will be four times as likely to die in any given year as a non–drinker of the same age, sex and economic status.

The effects of alcohol on an individual's health are difficult to overestimate.

It is common now for 20 per cent of all male admissions to general medical wards to be related to the use of alcohol. Many people still believe that the only organ likely to be damaged by drinking is the liver. Sadly, that is not true. People who drink heavily risk developing cancer, stomach ulcers and muscle wastage as well as liver disease. In France, where people drink more than anywhere else, 10 per cent of all deaths are directly due to the excessive consumption of alcohol.

Next, consider tobacco, another commonly used stress relieving drug.

Recently the Chief Medical Officer at the Department of Health and Social Security in Britain reported that smoking is 'by far the largest avoidable health hazard in Britain today and causes about 100,000 deaths in the UK each year'. A previous Chief Medical Officer at the DHSS once described the cigarette as 'the most lethal instrument devised by man for peaceful use'. In America the United States Surgeon General claims that tobacco is responsible for 340,000 deaths every year and the cost to American society, in terms of health care and lost production, was recently estimated at nearly $40,000,000,000 a year.

The list of diseases associated with tobacco smoking seems to grow annually. There are the respiratory disorders such as asthma and bronchitis. Chest infections are particularly common among smokers. Sinus troubles such as sinusitis and catarrh are caused or made worse by tobacco as are many gum and tooth disorders. Of the problems which affect the stomach, indigestion, gastritis and peptic ulcers have all been identified as being exacerbated by smoking. Many circulatory problems, raised blood pressure, arterial blockages and strokes are all known to be tobacco related.

Although there has been a slight fall in the number of people who smoke, there are still many millions who are addicted to tobacco and who use it to help them deal with stress and pressure.

Tranquillisers and sleeping tablets are the third group of commonly used stress relieving products. Experts now estimate that in Britain alone there are in excess of 3,000,000 people addicted to tranquillisers such as Valium, Librium and Ativan (also known under the chemical names diazepam, chlordiazepoxide and lorazepam) and sleeping tablets such as Mogadon (nitrazepam).

The picture is much the same in all other Western, developed countries.

The real problem is that these drugs are now widely thought to be more addictive and more damaging than illegal drugs such as heroin and cocaine. One eminent British psychiatrist recently announced that she would rather try to wean ten patients off heroin than one off tranquillisers.

Not that it is just the addictive nature of these drugs that causes problems. Researchers around the world have now also shown that these commonly prescribed tranquillisers and sleeping tablets (all members of a group of drugs known as the benzodiazepines) also cause an enormous number of side effects. So, for example, it is known that when taken for more than a few days they can cause serious memory loss, depression, anxiety and confusion. There seems little doubt that many millions of over-stressed individuals are living and working under the influence of these drugs.

Addiction to these three drugs — alcohol, tobacco and the benzodiazepine tranquillisers — leads to the loss of efficiency and effectiveness. It also leads to massive medical costs and absenteeism.

I estimate that in an average company 1 in every 4 members of the staff will be working below their best because of the 'drugs' they are taking.

5 PEOPLE UNDER PRESSURE — VULNERABLE SITUATIONS

I'VE ALREADY explained that not all individuals respond in exactly the same way to stress. One man's poisson is another man's poison and one man's stress is another man's pleasure. One of the major reasons why there are so many disputes and problems in industry is that so many managers, directors and executives assume that everyone thinks, feels and responds in exactly the same way. They don't.

In fact none of us responds to the same situation in the same way two days running. You cannot predict how people are going to respond to something unless you know as much as possible about them, their circumstances and what other pressures they may be under.

Think about this and you'll see it makes good sense. If you have a bad night's sleep and wake up late to find a pile of bills waiting for you then by the time you get in the car you'll be in a foul mood. The first motorist who cuts you up will get a rude gesture, a few poorly chosen words and a loud honk on the horn.

On the other hand if you sleep well after a splendid evening's entertainment and you wake up to find that you've won £100,000 in a lottery then you'll drive to work with a smile on your face and you'll respond generously to anyone who bumps into your car on the way to work.

Having said all that, it is nevertheless a fact that if you know what to look for you can pick out people who are particularly likely to be vulnerable to stressful situations.

We all *can* be vulnerable; but some people are more vulnerable than others!

Here are some of the individuals who are particularly likely to be susceptible to stress — and, more specifically, to be susceptible to change:

1. Anyone who has a low self-esteem will be exceptionally vulnerable. The man who has no real confidence will be constantly waiting for things to go wrong. He will be slow, hesitant, cautious and unwilling to take risks. Tragically, his very vulnerability will probably mean that he does make more mistakes. But give someone like this confidence and he will prove an excellent, reliable and loyal employee. A little praise, a nudge in the right direction occasionally and you'll have an excellent, faithful and competent employee.

2. It may sound obvious but you should look out for anyone who is going through a phase of personal readjustment. Anyone who has personal problems will be exceptionally vulnerable to problems at work. It is not uncommon for employees in this sort of situation to use an unstable, changing work situation as an excuse for all their own problems. If you don't keep them fully informed, tell them what is happening at work and show an interest in personal problems, then they may soon begin to behave unreasonably. And remember that not all personal crises are the obvious ones such as death or divorce. Many people — men and women — go through a personal mid–life crisis when they reach middle age. Every employee celebrating a fortieth birthday needs careful handling.

3. Obsessional individuals need routine. They suffer badly when things change. If you have an employee who is always neat and tidy, who is never late, whose work is always precise, whose desk is always ordered, then watch out during a departmental reorganisation. He is

probably the one person you think you can rely on. But if you don't give him a chance to control things then you may find him taking time off work — or even leaving. The best solution is to let him take charge of the reorganisation. Give him special responsibility for preparing a flow plan chart to show when everything has to be done.

4. You need to be particularly careful with people whose lives are empty in areas outside their work. The individual who takes his job very seriously, who has an unhappy or unsatisfying home life, or who lives with aged parents may suffer very badly if things change at work. He or she will feel threatened by the prospects of change. But tell them what is going on, explain that the planned changes will improve their future prospects and increase their level of security, and all will be well. Ignore them, tell them nothing and they'll be prime candidates for a nervous breakdown.

5. The employee who has worked for twenty years to become head of a department, whose whole life has been geared towards obtaining that particular post and who feels proud and pleased with his job will feel disappointed, cheated and threatened if departmental changes are suddenly planned. He will be particularly vulnerable if he believes that he has reached the peak of his own abilities and feels unsure of his ability to go further. Any change in his working circumstances will merely threaten to detract from his status rather than add to it.

6. The age of an employee can have a dramatic effect on his ability to cope with change. Anyone in his late forties, fifties or sixties will probably find it difficult to adapt to change and new rules. Some people are naturally better at adapting than others. Some people in this age group will welcome the idea of early retirement. That may be bad for your business. At a time of change you may well feel that you need workers with plenty of experience, good contacts or a breadth of knowledge of your business. If you want them to stay, talk to them as soon as you can and explain exactly what the future holds for the company and for them. Tell them why you need them and explain what 'old' values they can contribute to the new, improved business.

7. The more an individual enjoys his job the unhappier he or she will be at the prospect of change. There is a real risk that during a badly planned reorganisation you will lose all the best employees you have and keep the worst. If you don't explain properly why things will be better in the future, the people who are good at their jobs and who like what they do will probably look around for other posts. And because they are good at what they do they'll probably find new work without too much difficulty. You'll be left with the people you wished had gone — the people who know darned well that they'd find it difficult to get work elsewhere.

8. Watch out for the high flier — the socially mobile 'yuppie' who seems to be going places fast. He may be a valuable asset to the company. He may look like a tough, fast mover but he may well be one of the most vulnerable men in the whole company.

Anyone who is moving up the promotion ladder, earning more money, moving to a bigger house, driving a larger, more expensive car, increases his chances of having a heart attack three or four times. If he stretches himself financially by buying a house with a massive mortgage then his risks are even greater. And if he is under pressure at home or has a complicated love life then you can multiply his chances of having a heart attack another six times.

9. Watch out for anyone who takes over from a manager who was in a position for a long time. The 'new boy' may be resented by those staff members who think

that they should have been promoted. The 'old' manager may have been well loved and he may have done things in an inefficient sort of way. Changes in the department may be vital but without the right sort of support from above your new manager may succumb to the pressure.

10.   Anyone 'in the middle' of any sort of company hierarchy is inevitably vulnerable. But he will be particularly vulnerable when the flow of information downwards stops or is too miserly. Consider, for example, the case of Ronald Braithwaite, a foreman at a factory making roofing panels. He was, by all accounts, good at his job. Moreover, he had managed to remain balanced on the narrow tightrope that stretches between management and shop floor. (The factory foreman has one of the most difficult jobs in industry — it is easy for him to be despised both by the office managers who give him instructions and the workers on the shop floor who take orders from him. Obtaining and keeping the respect of these two quite different groups requires a very special kind of skill.)

Everything went well until a rumour started to go round that the company was to be taken over by a large German timber group. Naturally the workmen wanted to know what was going on. They wanted to know if their jobs were safe. Ronald asked the Production Manager but could find out nothing. He told the men that he didn't know what was happening but they didn't believe him and grew more and more restless. When I first saw him he was getting angina pains that showed as clear as daylight that he was suffering from the stress he was under.

Ronald insisted on staying at work and begged the Production Manager for information. But he got nothing. By this time Ronald wasn't just worried by the questions he couldn't answer but he was worried about his own future. He had a heart attack.

The truth was that a German company had made a bid but the bid had been turned down. There wasn't anything particularly complicated about it and there wasn't any great secrecy about what had happened. Anyone reading the city pages of any large national newspaper would have known what was going on. The Production Manager had decided not to tell Ronald because he didn't want 'to worry the men'.

His failure to understand that you can't squash rumours with silence, and that you can't ease fears and anxieties without information, had led to Ronald's heart attack. It cost Ronald his health. It cost the company the services of an excellent foreman.

6 STRESS-PRODUCING CIRCUMSTANCES

JUST AS some individuals are far more vulnerable to stress than others, so there are some circumstances which seem especially likely to provoke confusion, controversy and consternation.

The list that follows is by no means comprehensive, but will give you an idea of how some common situations can provoke stress reactions.

1. Takeovers and mergers are extremely stressful for everyone in a company — not just the executives or directors who are actually handling the deal. Takeovers can alter the established company pecking order, remove prestige, lower earnings, destroy well established, much loved routines, reduce job satisfaction and so on. Few situations are as threatening or as frightening as a takeover. And the best way to minimise the amount of stress that is spread around is to provide everyone concerned with as much information as possible.

One of the biggest problems associated with a takeover is not what *will* happen but what people *fear* will happen. You can't remove all fears and suspicions with accurate information but you can remove the fears and suspicions that are based on rumour rather than fact. Remember, too, that to many employees the merger of two departments can be just as threatening and as stressful as the merger of two separate companies.

2. Shift work is common in many industries —

particularly those where expensive machinery is employed (the car and computer industry); where international times have to be followed (the money markets); where round the clock working is essential to prevent problems developing from a rundown (for example in the steel industry); in service industries (transport and hospitals); or where the nature of the product is such that out of hours work is essential (newspaper production).

Some employees have no choice about shift work — it is part of their working pattern. But others are attracted to it by higher wages, more time off, longer holidays or simply by the opportunity to have more daylight hours free for their own activities.

Whatever the motivation may be, it is always vitally important to remember that shift work (particularly when working at night) affects the body in a number of ways. Sleep disturbances and appetite disturbances are common physical manifestations of this particular type of stress, but family problems and social and sexual anxieties are also common. Unless the motivation is great enough (and the reward convincing enough), the individual on shift work is exceptionally vulnerable to stress due to change or fear.

Finally, it is perhaps also worth pointing out that individuals who work shifts are particularly likely to suffer from a shortage of information. Isolated as they are from normal working life they often get their information through rumour and gossip. A weekly or monthly newsletter, filled with facts about new appointments, new working schemes, product changes, sales successes, new contracts and plans for the future can improve morale and efficiency considerably. Failing a newsletter, a simple bulletin board, updated regularly, is an excellent idea.

3. Most company executives spend a considerable amount of time travelling. Many executives spend most of their time travelling. And, of course, these days most

executives do most of their long distance travelling in aeroplanes.

Although the term 'jet lag' is now used commonly, the extent of the disruption of physiological and psychological rhythms that is caused by air travel is still underestimated. Nor is it widely realised that the disturbance produced by flying long distances can easily lead to a much enhanced susceptibility to stress. The experts claim that for each time zone a traveller goes through he should allow a day for recovery.

The common symptoms of jet lag include an inability to get to sleep, altered eating patterns, disturbed bowel habits and reduced mental and physical efficiency. Any executive who bravely insists on pushing himself along without giving his body a chance to adjust to the change is likely to make bad decisions, to offend people and to damage his own health.

Apart from insisting that anyone travelling by plane rests before starting business negotiations, there are several ways in which the disturbances produced by flying can be minimised:

(a) Try to avoid anything other than very light snacks on the plane and avoid all heavy meals for 24 hours before flying.

(b) The body clock finds it easier to cope if you take off in the morning and arrive at your destination in the evening. Flying overnight can be particularly disruptive. An additional advantage of arriving at night is that you will almost certainly have a chance to get at least one good night's sleep before beginning negotiations.

(c) Dehydration can contribute to jet lag, so drink plenty of water on the plane. Avoid strong coffee or tea (the caffeine can make things worse) and avoid too much alcohol. Champagne is particularly likely to cause problems. If you need a glass of something, stick to malt whisky with water. Don't mix spirits and wine.

(d) Try to sleep as much as you can on the plane. Use

a mask to cover your eyes. It is a good idea to write on it a simple message such as 'Please do not wake for meals'.

(e) If you have real power you can, of course, simply insist on sticking to your local home time wherever you are. Former U.S. President Lyndon B. Johnson once held a conference in Guam and conducted the whole three-day affair at White House time. His team was constantly fresh, while the other delegates, from different time zones, were jet lagged into submission.

4. Every year thousands of executives and other employees go abroad to work for their companies. And every year thousands of people have to come back home again because they can't cope with the pressure. A staggering one third of the people sent to work abroad have to return home because of ill health, alcoholism, a failure to cope or a simple breakdown. Most of those problems are a direct result of an inability to cope with the stress of working overseas.

Since at a conservative estimate (that doesn't include the cost of efficiency and goodwill) it costs £50,000 to replace a 'failed' expatriate, it is clearly important to try and ensure that employees working abroad do not 'crack up'.

Here are some pointers that should help reduce the likelihood of executive stress in an expatriate:

(a) Choose carefully before selecting people to work abroad. There is a tremendous tendency for companies to send misfits or problem employees abroad. That is crazy. It is asking for trouble. Similarly, there is a tendency for people who can't cope at home to volunteer for an over-seas posting in the hope that things will turn out better. That, too, is likely to prove disastrous. The selection procedures for overseas postings need to be particularly strict.

(b) Anyone going to work abroad should be warned about what to expect in the way of climate changes (how hot or how cold does it really get?), language barriers (how many natives speak English and how difficult is it to learn the local language?), religious customs (in some countries women aren't allowed out alone, aren't allowed out in trousers and no one can drink alcohol even in private) and the problems of finding schools or good health care facilities.

(c) Anyone going to work abroad will inevitably have to say goodbye to family and friends for long periods of time. There is a real risk that anyone working abroad will feel alienated from both the parent company and the locals. People working abroad need to be exceptionally strong willed and self confident in order to cope with these exceptional stresses. They need to be able to cope with stress without 'crutches' such as alcohol or tobacco and they need to be able to get on with all sorts of people very easily.

(d) It is important to make sure that anyone going to work abroad has a great capacity for change and can cope easily with pressures and stresses of all kinds. Make sure that he or she understands exactly how long the assign-ment will last and exactly what the future may hold. Employees should have access to colleagues and superiors with whom they can discuss difficulties. Free time should be respected. Expectations and roles should be clearly defined. The company should provide facilities for rest and recreation. The company should also provide feed-back so that the expatriate knows that his work is being appreciated and well received. It is vitally important that the expatriate be kept well informed about company policy and company plans.

Nothing is more likely to devastate local morale than a rumour brought in by a peripatetic competitor that suggests problems or imminent changes back home.

(e) Finally, it is vital to remember that for an expatriate who has been abroad for over a year, resettling back home can be extremely difficult. The company culture may have changed. Friends and colleagues will have moved on and there will be financial and social problems to face. Coming back home can often lead to a fall in living standards. There will be tax problems, housing difficulties and there may be a reduction in status.

All these problems can be overcome — but only with some thought.

5. All executives should remember that moving house is one of the most stressful and potentially harmful experiences any of us can go through. It can be just as devastating as divorce or bereavement.

Most large companies now recognise that moving home is an expensive business — and most will, therefore, make some financial contribution when an employee has to be moved.

Lawyers' bills, estate agents' fees, taxes and removal company bills are only a small part of the overall cost. There will probably be new carpets and curtains to be bought and it may even be necessary to buy new furniture.

But the financial cost of moving home is only part of the problem.

There are social and personal problems to be overcome. Friends and relatives have to be left behind; new schools have to be found and the problem of finding a suitable new home may cause endless stress and unhappiness. Many employees who move to a different part of the same country end up spending weeks separated from their families. Even when separation is avoided whole families sometimes have to live in hotels.

Executives responsible for moving employees around within the same country should always try to give employees a choice about whether to move or not. They should always make it clear why the move is necessary and what benefits will ensue — both to the company and to the individual who is moving.

Stress can be produced by an apparently endless number

of situations. It can be caused by poor working relationships, by too much responsibility, by too little responsibility, by frustration, by boredom, by too little money, by fear about the future, by change that seems threatening, by new technology, by having too much to do and by having too little to do.

We humans are fallible and delicate creatures. Our minds ensure that we are vulnerable to fears and anxieties which are often more hypothetical than practical. We worry about what may happen as well as what will happen or what has already happened. Our responses to an imagined future can be just as violent and destructive as our responses to things that have happened in the past.

Of course, stress doesn't just arise in an industrial situation. We are all exposed to stress in our personal, private lives. Our own fears, hopes, aspirations and ambitions can all lead to anxiety and to stress related diseases. Problems with our families and friends can result in exactly the same sort of physiological response produced by problems at work. The same applies to anxieties about a hobby, or about a sporting endeavour.

But wherever it arises, whatever the fundamental cause of it may be, in the end all unwanted, excessive stress has an adverse effect on the individual's ability to work competently, efficiently, effectively and continuously.

Part 3

MANAGING PEOPLE FOR HEALTHY PROFITS

Read each of the following sections carefully — and re-read them even more carefully. If you follow the advice they contain, the employees in your company will suffer far less from stress.

And because they are happy — and are working better — you will benefit too.

None of the advice here will cost your company much (if anything) in terms of money; none of the advice will cost you much in terms of time or effort.

But within months you'll notice the difference; your company will be more efficient, personnel problems will be greatly reduced, and profits will increase.

GIVE PEOPLE AS MUCH RESPONSIBILITY AS THEY CAN SAFELY HANDLE

You undoubtedly know that over-promoting employees is a common cause of problems. But you may not realise that just as many stress related problems are caused by under-promotion as by over-promotion.

Try to give your employees as much responsibility as you think they can safely handle. Gradually increase the amount of responsibility you give them until you reach the maximum point of comfort.

An American telephone company in a large town employed a dozen women to prepare telephone directories for publication. The women all worked together on the whole project, sharing the general responsibility for the work they were doing. The directories were full of errors — subscribers were omitted, names were spelt wrongly and there were numerous complaints.

Then someone had a brainwave. Each woman was given the responsibility for producing an individual telephone directory. Each woman became 'editor' of her 'own' telephone book.

The improvement was staggering. The number of mistakes in each directory fell dramatically. The turnover of staff also fell. And the number of days lost through sickness dropped.

The work hadn't changed at all. But by dividing it up in a different way, and sharing the responsibility individually rather than collectively, efficiency improved considerably.

By and large the more responsibility you give people the more responsible they will be.

REMEMBER TO SAY THANK YOU

I attended a massive, international conference not long ago. It was a huge success. Delegates had flown in from all over the world and they were delighted with all the arrangements. The lectures were useful and informative. The hotel accommodation was excellent. The food was delicious. And the evening entertainments were well planned and brilliantly executed.

The whole conference had been organised by a professional conference company. But a fairly junior executive of the sponsoring company had been given the job of liaising with the conference organisers. He had worked day and night for six months to ensure that everything was a success. His marriage had been put under an extraordinary strain.

On the last evening of the conference I found the junior executive in a dark corner of the hotel bar. He was alone and quietly getting drunk.

When I asked him what the matter was and why he wasn't joining in the final evening celebrations he told me that he was thinking of leaving his company. He said he never wanted to see the Chairman again.

Knowing that the directors had been extremely pleased with the executive's work — and that they all felt the conference had been a great success — I was surprised. I asked him why he felt so low.

'I've just been given my next assignment,' the executive sobbed into his brandy. 'The Chairman wants me to help set up a new Overseas Marketing Unit. It's a good job I guess. But do you know I've just put six months of my life into this conference and I didn't even get a "thank you"?'

That was what was hurting.

No one had said 'Thank you' or 'Well done'.

You can give a man a better job. You can give him a pay rise. You can give him a bigger car, a bigger office and a flashier secretary. But nothing replaces a quiet 'Well done' and an honest, old fashioned 'Thank you'.

KNOW WHEN TO PUSH — AND WHEN TO STOP

It's one of the most important secrets of good management: knowing when to push hard and when to stop pushing.

You have to push hard to get the best out of people. Everyone knows that. But pushing too hard can be counterproductive.

Too many managers use their staff carelessly and without thought.

Think carefully: are you ever guilty of pushing your staff too hard?

Whipping a donkey doesn't do any good if the donkey is already going as fast as it can.

SMILE AND THE WORLD WILL SMILE WITH YOU

Try this simple experiment: smile at someone every time he uses a particular word. You'll discover that he will unconsciously use that particular word more and more often. He'll be getting an appreciative response from you and he'll respond accordingly. He won't know why he is doing it, but he'll want to please you, and see you smile, and so he'll keep on doing it.

Similarly, if you smile at someone every time he does something you want him to keep on doing you'll find that he keeps repeating the action.

He may not know why he is doing it and he may not even know that he is repeating himself. But he'll keep on because it feels good.

Even the man who thinks of himself as extremely macho and aggressive wants to please people. It is a natural human emotion.

Mothers, lovers and good salesmen have for years relied on this natural response. They smile at their children, their partners and their customers. And they get better results.

But, amazingly, most managers never bother.

The evidence all shows that the more you smile at someone (within obvious limits) the more he will like you and want to do things for you. If you smile at people when they are working well, and withold your smiles when they are not working well, then efficiency will improve.

There is also a bonus. If you smile more often you'll find that you feel better too.

A smile from you every morning will increase productivity and reduce absenteeism.

TAKE THE TERROR OUT OF COMPUTERISATION

Computerisation is to the industrial revolution what the industrial revolution was to the agricultural revolution — a fundamental transformation of methods of production and consumption and a major change in life itself.

Things that we don't properly understand are always worrying, and few things seem to worry the average employee as much as computers. Let a rumour spread that you're about to computerise the firm's accounts department or that you are inviting a computer expert to visit the company with a view to introducing a modernisation programme and the collective blood pressure of the workforce will rise dramatically.

Because computers often pose a threat and frighten us we respond to their presence in much the same way as we would respond to the presence of a wild animal.

Take a wild tiger into the accounts department and you wouldn't be surprised if people's heart rates went up, if their blood pressures rose, if they acquired headaches caused by muscle tension and if they developed acid indigestion.

But to the 20th century employee a computer can produce exactly the same sort of physical response. It is a threat to his existence and his security. Moreover, it doesn't disappear after a few hours. It is still there tomorrow and the day after.

To you a computer may be a terrific acquisition. To another employee it may be simply terrifying.

People worry about computers for a number of reasons. They worry that the computer will take over their work. They worry that the computer will make them redundant. They worry that the computer will make their lives more boring.

There are a number of ways in which you can introduce

computer technology without scaring the life out of employees. Here are a few simple rules to follow:

1. Explain that you don't have to know how a computer works in order to use one. Point out that millions of people drive cars, watch television and turn on electric light bulbs without having the faintest notion about how any of those things work.

2. Point out that computers can help do the most boring work. They can do the dull, mind boggling, repetitive tasks that no one likes. They can take the tedium out of many types of office work and free employees for more creative, satisfying work.

3. If a computer is going to make some people redundant then be honest. Tell everyone exactly what plans there are for redundancies. But assure remaining employees that the computer will not threaten their jobs. If you try to disguise the truth then the damage done by the rumours, suspicions and fears will undoubtedly exceed the damage done by the planned changes.

4. Remind people that computers are neither infallible nor stupid. Computers cannot think. Computers are often accused of making mistakes (everyone has heard of the gas board computer which sent a little old lady a bill for a million pounds) but in fact, of course, it is the programmer not the computer that makes the mistakes. The computer isn't bright enough to make mistakes.

5. Remember that computers can increase the throughput of work — and consequently increase company profitability and prospects for everyone.

6. Program a sense of humour into the computer. Most company computers are incredibly boring. But they needn't be. With a little skill a computer can be programmed to talk back to individuals who try to tease it or make fun of it. Program in jokes and birthday greetings. The more 'human' you make a computer the more readily it will be accepted.

Having a new computer in an office is like having a wild animal sitting in a corner of the room. The physical and mental consequences can be just as devastating.

DON'T UNDERESTIMATE THE PERIL OF BOREDOM

We tend to think of stress and pressure as being caused by too much activity. But inactivity and boredom can be just as great a cause of stress and can cause all the physical and mental problems associated with having too much to do. Henry Ford, who may have been a great car manufacturer, but wasn't always too bright, once claimed that people never want to think at work. He used to encourage them to hang up their minds in the cloakroom — or, preferably, to leave them in the car park outside!

He was wrong. Repetitive, boring, routine work causes errors, inefficiency, disputes, absenteeism and ill health. It is often boredom that drives people to drink too much or to take drugs.

And yet despite the existence of powerful evidence showing the problems associated with boredom, there are millions of people around today whose work demands nothing more than that they act as nursemaids to expensive, complicated pieces of machinery which they do not understand.

In factories there are pieces of machinery which can turn out finely finished objects no craftsman working with his own hands and tools could hope to emulate.

In offices there are computers and word processors

which can write letters, check spelling and keep files far more speedily and efficiently than any individual could hope to.

These days, machines are so sophisticated that they too often become the principals in any working relationship. The individual is left too little opportunity for pride or self expression.

There are, however, a number of things that you can do to minimise the damage done by boredom in your company.

1.   Always try to design jobs with people in mind. Don't just hire people to look after machines. Remember that people are a basic stock resource. If you use your people properly and treat them well then you will make better use of all your other resources.

2.   Try to ensure that repetitive or monotonous tasks are spread around as much as possible.

3.   Assembly lines were popular twenty or thirty years ago but in recent years numerous large companies have shown that sharing work and responsibility around in a more 'humane' manner increases the overall efficiency and productivity of the company.

Car companies have shown that product quality goes up, absenteeism goes down and productivity rises when assembly lines are disassembled and workers are divided into groups and given the responsibility for producing individual vehicles.

4.   Remember that it isn't just factory staff who can be affected by boredom. Office workers — and executives too — can all suffer in exactly the same way. Try to ensure that people's ambitions are not thwarted, that their talents are not suppressed and that their hopes are not squashed.

5.   When individual workers are bored, look for new ways to add more responsibility to their lives while at the same time benefitting the company. So, for example,

petrol station attendants can be encouraged to undertake market research work that adds interest to their working lives. The information they acquire will then help the company plan for the future.

An industrial rut can easily become a slough of despond.

TEACH PEOPLE TO ACCEPT CHANGE

We are living in a world of constant change. And every time something changes, someone, somewhere, gets heartburn.

These days the half life of technical knowledge is between three and five years. The result is that hundreds of thousands of technicians who think they are in the vanguard of science will need retraining every year. Thousands of experts who think they understand computers are already out of date.

People are frightened of change for a host of different reasons.

They are frightened because when things change, jobs disappear.

They are frightened because when things change, job satisfaction sometimes goes out of the window.

They are frightened because they may end up with too much responsibility.

They are frightened because they may end up with too little reponsibility, doing boring jobs as machine minders.

They are frightened that they may not have the necessary skills to enable them to adapt to the changes.

Amidst all this fear there are other emotions. People resent changes they have no control over. They worry that the change may result in the organisation failing.

They are angry because skills they struggled to acquire are suddenly worthless. When people who have acquired manual skills discover these skills are to be made redundant overnight by technological change it is hardly surprising that they respond with what outsiders sometimes regard as a Luddite mentality.

Remember, too, that cerebral skills can also be taken over by machines that can do the work quicker, more efficiently and more economically.

These are all unalterable and inescapable facts. But with thought and care it is possible to minimise the damage done by the inevitable and necessary change.

Employees must never be allowed to forget that human beings have many skills and assets which cannot be replaced by machines. However complex and efficient new machines may be, people will always be essential.

It is vitally important to make sure that no one is ever employed to 'mind' a machine. Machines should always be introduced to make jobs easier or more efficient. People must always know that they are more important than the machines they work with. The man, not the machine, is the principal partner in any relationship.

Be honest about the strengths and weaknesses of changes you are introducing. Point out how the new machines will offer the possibility of better working conditions and more work satisfaction.

AVOID TOO MUCH ADMINISTRATION

Administrators and bureaucrats have no primary functions. By themselves they have no status and no *raison d'être*. You cannot run a company with bureaucrats and administrators alone.

But once a company has reached a critical size, the number (and power) of its internal bureaucracies can easily get out of control.

Instead of existing merely to ensure that the creative and productive aspects of the business function effectively and efficiently the bureaucracy will begin to acquire a new, special status of its own. And it will start to grow.

You can see this law in operation in any branch of the Civil Service and throughout the nationalised industries.

When a company's administrators begin to think of themselves as having an independent function and value, the consequences can be dire. Instead of functioning to make and sell paperclips, cars or insurance the company will suddenly exist to feed its own bureaucratic machinery.

Those in the company who have a creative function will lose heart. Those whose jobs are in practical production will despair.

It is vital to remember the purpose of the company. A close eye should always be kept on the size of the company's bureaucracy. Not just because bureaucracies cost money, but also because overlarge bureaucracies depress and stress those upon whose shoulders the company's financial strengths are built.

Storekeepers, cooks and transport chiefs are an essential part of any army. But it's the fighting soldiers who win battles.

TEACH EMPLOYEES TO RECOGNISE THEIR OWN STRESS SIGNS

In order to tell when symptoms are developing, all an individual needs is an awareness of the sort of signs which show that stress is causing problems.

Most of us have a particular weak spot and once we know what that is we can learn to spot our own 'early warning signs' very speedily. The common 'early warning signs' (which show when someone is pushing himself too hard — or being pushed too hard) are very simple. The physical signs of early stress can, for example, include a headache, indigestion and an inability to get to sleep at night.

As an employer you will be able to spot when your employees are being pushed too hard simply by watching out for telltale symptoms. The salesman who suddenly starts swigging white antacid three times a day has a problem. The accounts clerk who is promoted and who then has every Friday afternoon off with a migraine is being pushed beyond her comfortable limits. The account executive who is given a big job and inexplicably gets more and more irritable at work is probably suffering from too much stress.

The closer you are to your employees the better able you will be to spot the early signs of distress. But however close to them you get, you will never be quite as capable of spotting their early signs of distress as they themselves will be — if you first teach them what to look out for.

The best psychologist in the world can't spot unbearable stress as quickly as the individual concerned.

NEVER GIVE AUTHORITY WITHOUT RESPONSIBILITY AND NEVER GIVE RESPONSIBILITY WITHOUT AUTHORITY

Engrave this simple rule on your heart!

When I was a general practitioner I knew two patients who proved the dangers of ignoring this rule.

The first patient was a car park attendant. He was the classic 'man in a uniform'. He would have made an excellent traffic warden if he hadn't remained in the private sector.

He had a modestly paid job but he had quite a lot of authority and absolutely no responsibility. His job was to look after the company car park and to prevent unauthorised members of the public from parking there. There was a large supermarket only a hundred yards or so from the factory and many shoppers had taken to leaving their cars in the company car park while filling their shopping trolleys at the supermarket.

The result was that staff members couldn't get into the car park and there were abandoned shopping trolleys lying discarded around the place.

Problems arose with the company's sales representatives who should have had passes to the car park but rarely did. The result was chaos.

The attendant, following his instructions to the letter, steadfastly refused to allow the salesmen into the car park when they arrived without their passes. He had the authority to refuse anyone admission and he refused to see this rule broken. He had been given ample authority for the job but no responsibility to use his discretion.

Not surprisingly, the sales representatives didn't take too kindly to being forced to find parking spaces in the street outside. They were always angry and invariably abusive. The car park attendant coped well with it for a couple of weeks but by the time he came to see me he couldn't relax, couldn't sleep and had all the signs of a developing duodenal ulcer.

His problem was only solved when he was given *responsibility* to go with his authority.

The patient who displayed problems acquired from having too much responsibility and not enough authority was a practice manager who worked for another GP.

Her problem was that her employers expected her to handle all the administrative and management aspects of the practice but resolutely refused to give her any of the authority she needed to do the job properly.

She was expected to reprimand receptionists if they didn't do their jobs correctly. She was expected to inform them about new changes and to coordinate their holidays and working rotas. But she didn't have any clear authority over the staff at all. (Oddly enough she wasn't as interested in getting more money as she was in getting the status she needed to do her job properly).

The inevitable problems she found herself struggling to deal with gave her more or less constant migraine headaches.

But once she had managed to persuade her employer to give her the status she needed, her migraine headaches completely disappeared.

Authority and responsibility go together like day and night. You really can't have one without the other.

TREAT PEOPLE AS PEOPLE — NOT TOOLS

When the boss of Sony was asked the secret of employee loyalty his answer was simple.

'Never treat employees as tools', was his reply.

And yet in many companies that is exactly what does happen. Employees are treated as mere pathways to profit. It is hardly surprising that they get to work at the latest possible moment, leave at the earliest possible moment, and do as little as they can in between.

By treating people as people, employers really can benefit.

A man I know owns several petrol stations. Like many people in the same business he has a high staff turnover.

He just can't keep new assistants. As soon as he's trained one she gets bored and fed up with the work and leaves to get a job somewhere else — not necessarily for more money. Advertising for and training new staff costs him a fortune.

At least that *used* to be the case. For, thanks to a lucky break, he has solved his staff turnover problem.

He was ordering a new set of lapel name badges for his latest set of recruits when the chap selling the badges apologetically told him that they were right out of badges and were likely to be out of 'blanks' for another month or so. It was the usual excuse — trouble at the suppliers.

'But,' suggested the bright salesman at the other end of the telephone, 'why not order some desk name plates?'

And so, instead of having 'Daphne', 'Enid' and 'Helen' printed on small white plastic lapel badges the petrol station owner ordered the same names on free standing plastic name plates that measured 10 inches by 2 inches.

To his astonishment the assistants loved the name plates. And before he knew what was happening one of them had persuaded him to have even bigger name plates made and suspended from the ceiling above their counters.

Each time one of the girls came on duty she put up her own name plate and the service station became known as 'Daphne's' or 'Enid's' or 'Helen's'. The other girls quickly insisted on having their own name plates made up too.

The owner soon noticed a pleasant side effect: business started to get better. The girls took a much greater interest in the stock they were carrying. They asked for (and got) smart, matching uniforms. They asked for (and got) a small hair and make up allowance. They took a real pride in what they were doing.

And they didn't leave after a few months. They wanted to stay.

It isn't difficult to see why such a small change should have such a large effect.

When Daphne pins a name label on her overalls she is

merely identifying herself as part of the surroundings. She, like the sweets, soft drinks and crisp displays, is labelled as a product.

But when she hangs her name plate over the counter she is taking over her environment. It is (temporarily) her territory. She has status. She is identified. She isn't just another number on the payroll. She is someone important. And so naturally she takes a pride in her work. She wants to do well. She smiles at the customers. She encourages them to spend.

And the end result is, of course, that the customers are happier too. They come back as regulars. They spend more money on sweets, tobacco and motoring accessories.

The garage owner has become a richer and happier man. And because he worries less and has less stress he is fitter too.

If you treat people as tools they'll screw up your profits.

TEACH PEOPLE TO SAY NO

'No' is one of the most difficult words to say in the English language.

Not being able to say no leads us into all sorts of difficult and painful personal circumstances.

It results in unwanted pregnancies, commitments we can't cope with and dinner parties that are a real bore.

But not being able to say no also leads to a wide range of commercial problems and pressures too.

It leads to your company being committed to projects and partners which are neither suitable nor profitable.

It leads to people buying materials that are substandard or not needed.

It leads to agreements and contracts which prove embarrassing and costly.

We say yes when we really mean no for all sorts of reasons.

We say yes because we have been put under pressure. We are blackmailed into saying yes. We say yes because we are vain and want to appear strong and decisive. We say yes because we are frightened of what people might say if we say no. We say yes because someone else has said yes. We say yes because we want to please the person who wants us to say yes.

To reduce long term business stress teach your employees that there is nothing wrong in thinking about decisions. Teach them that there is nothing 'wimpish' about delaying decision making until you've got all the facts. Teach people that asking for a few minutes to think about an offer is a sign of strength not weakness.

More people go bankrupt through saying yes too often than go bankrupt through saying no too often.

MAKE SURE THAT PEOPLE HAVE PROPER CONTROL OVER THE MACHINERY THEY USE

The more complicated machinery becomes the more likely it is to go wrong and the more likely it is that the person operating it will not be able to mend it.

This sort of stress has been common in the home for years. Today a housewife is dependent upon a great variety of machines. There is the washing machine, the vacuum cleaner, the food mixer, the spin drier, the dish washer and so on. If just one of these machines goes wrong the consequences can be disastrous for two reasons.

First, the housewife may not have any simple backup alternatives. There is a chance that she won't own a washing line on which to dry her clothes. She may not have a dustpan and brush. She may not even have a tea towel.

Secondly, the housewife cannot mend things that have broken. If her washing line broke she could easily mend it or, for a modest outlay, but a new one. If a spin drier or tumble drier breaks down it may take days or weeks before an engineer can be found — and the cost of the repairs will probably be horrendous.

Very much the same sort of thing happens in industry. And similar stresses result.

Old fashioned typewriters didn't break down too often but when they did there was nearly always someone around the office who could cope with the repair work.

Computers and word processors break down regularly. And when they do break down experts are needed to put them right. The result can be missed deadlines and all sorts of stresses and strains.

When taking advantage of new technology to improve the efficiency of your company you should take care to ensure that the necessary back-up maintenance specialists are constantly available. In addition, you should try to ensure that everyone operating a complex machine knows at least something about how the machine operates and the simple, common causes of the machine not working.

How often does an office close down for four hours because a ribbon has been put into a machine the wrong way round or because a photocopier has been jammed with a loose sheet of paper? Simple problems like these can often be prevented by proper staff training. Engineer call-outs and office closedowns can be avoided by teaching employees how to deal with the simpler, more common problems.

Everyone who operates a machine should know exactly what to do — or where to get help — if something goes wrong.

HELP EMPLOYEES PREPARE FOR RETIREMENT

I am constantly astonished by the number of companies which do nothing at all to prepare their employees for retirement.

At the age of 64 years and 364 days, George is a much loved and valued employee. Then, suddenly, 24 hours later, he gets a farewell party and a presentation clock. He becomes a pensioner.

Overnight he loses authority, power, responsibility, status and money. The meaning goes out of his life and he suddenly finds himself face to face with the problems that being a pensioner entails in our society.

Suddenly his life lacks meaning and purpose. He has no reason to get up in the morning. His friends live in another world. He is shunted into an anteroom to death and expected to entertain himself with his gold watch and his farewell cards.

Is it any wonder that men and women who suddenly retire often die within weeks of cashing in their last pay cheque?

Of course, it isn't only at retirement that retirement worries appear.

Most people start worrying about what retirement will mean to them anything up to ten or fifteen years before they get round to hanging up their boots.

They worry about how they will fill all the hours they will have to themselves. They worry about how they will cope without a regular earned income. They worry about the loneliness and sadness that seem to be for so many an inevitable part of retirement.

And, of course, people who worry do not work well. The individual who is having to retire against his will and who sees nothing ahead of him that he likes will feel aggrieved and bitter. Aggrieved, bitter employees do not work well.

By providing simple, straightforward advice for people who are about to retire you can help avoid most of these fears and anxieties. You can ensure that people look forward to retirement as another, exciting era in their lives. You can ensure that love and respect for the company remain unsullied.

And you can ensure that in the years approaching retirement the 50 and 60 year old works happily and enthusiastically.

The man who is concerned about the future will not be able to give his best for the present.

DEMOCRACY RULES OK!

How does your company decide whether or not a particular office becomes a 'no smoking' area?

If it is the sort of decision made by someone in management then your company is oppressing its employees and building up problems for the future.

The 'no smoking office' question is the sort of query that can only be answered satisfactorily by the employees who work in that office. Invite everyone who works full time in each office to vote. And then use management authority to see that the result of the vote is upheld.

This is not only an honourable and democratic way to

operate but it is also a simple way of ensuring that employees realise that they are part of the company, and not just hired hands who have no entitlement to a say in how their working conditions are controlled.

Unless you respect people's rights they won't respect your company.

ENCOURAGE FORGIVENESS AND DISCOURAGE GRUDGES

I once worked as an adviser to a medium sized factory in the Midlands where the two working directors didn't speak to one another. It was a bizarre situation because all communication between the two men had to be relayed through their secretaries.

'Tell Mr Y that we've got an order for 5,000 grommets from Blenkinsops,' Mr X would say to his secretary.

'Would you please tell Mr Y that we've got an order for 5,000 grommets from Blenkinsops,' Mr X's secretary would say to Mr Y's secretary.

'Mr X says that we've got an order for 5,000 grommets from Blenkinsops,' Mr Y's secretary would say to Mr Y.

'Do they want the quarter inch or the half inch?' Mr Y would ask his secretary.

'Mr Y wants to know if they want the quarter inch or the half inch,' Mr Y's secretary would say to Mr X's secretary.

'Mr Y wants to know if they want the quarter inch or the half inch,' Mr X's secretary would say to Mr X.

And so it went on. For year after year after year.

It must have cost the company thousands in wasted time, and lost orders.

And do you know why they didn't speak?

Because in 1957 Mr X had parked in Mr Y's car park space and had refused to move his car until he went home at lunchtime.

Few things will damage your profits as much as a good grudge.

ENCOURAGE INDEPENDENCE

Michael James had worked for his company (a large international retail group with branches around the world) for all his adult life. He had started off as an accounts clerk and risen to a powerful position as manager of one of the company's largest and most prestigious stores.

The company that Michael worked for had a reputation for taking particularly good care of its employees. But what many outsiders, myself included, didn't understand was that the company policy of taking good care of its employees wasn't entirely unselfish.

The fact is that the company wasn't just interested in helping its employees — it wanted to own them lock, stock and barrel.

Every aspect of Michael's life was run by his company. His large, comfortable, expensive, suburban home had been bought with the aid of a generous mortgage from the company. His two children were attending private schools where their fees were paid by a scholarship from the company. His wife's car was on loan from the company. And his pension plan and personal sickness plan were both done through the company too.

For years Michael had been untroubled by all this. His first realisation of just how much his life depended on the company came when there was a stock exchange rumour that the company was about to be taken over. Michael realised that if they were taken over and he lost his job, he would also lose his home, both his cars, his pension and his sickness insurance. His two sons would have to leave school and the house would have to be sold.

From that day on Michael never really felt comfortable again. He had suddenly become aware that being totally dependent on his company left him extremely vulnerable.

That vulnerability affected both his ability to work comfortably and his loyalty to the company.

There used to be a theory (it was particularly popular among managers working for large American corporations) that it was in a company's best interests to keep its employees totally dependent.

It was this philosophy which led to companies lending employees money for large mortgages at very preferential rates. It was this philosophy which led to companies offering all sorts of special perks such as complicated pension schemes, sickness benefits, paid school fees and subsidised holidays. And it was this philosophy which led to complicated share option schemes.

The theory was that if you kept your employees dependent then they would work harder and harder for the company, partly because they would be grateful and partly because they would be too frightened of the consequences if they didn't.

It was thought that the more employees were encouraged to depend on the company for everything, the less likely they would be to move elsewhere.

Those who were advocates of this particular theory were wrong.

When an employee becomes totally dependent on a company he becomes exceptionally vulnerable to fears and anxieties about his future. He worries too much about what will happen if something goes wrong. He worries about almost everything because the company controls his whole life. He knows only too well that a takeover, a merger or a change in company policy could result not just in losing a job but in his life being devastated.

To minimise the amount of stress employees are under, a company should play an important part in their lives, but it should not be the only thing in their lives. Nor should it control their lives.

A very dependent employee is often a very nervous employee. And a nervous employee does not work well.

TEACH EMPLOYEES TO ASK FOR HELP

Many employees (particularly the younger ones) will not realise that by asking for help and information they can learn, avoid problems, improve their efficiency and make more money for the company.

There is a good chance they will also not realise that asking for help and information can greatly reduce the level of their own stress.

They will fear that if they are seen to ask for advice and help they will be thought of as weak and uncertain.

They will fear that if they are seen asking for help they will be exhibiting their ignorance and weakening their future in the company.

That is a great pity. By asking for help, advice and information we can all help ourselves and those for whom we work. No one can know everything. We all need to acquire a constant supply of new information. We all need advice from people who have 'been there before.'

Encourage employees to talk to one another, to ask for and generously to give advice.

Everyone can benefit in this way. The younger

employee can gain from the experience of the older employee. And the older employee can gain from the younger employee's greater awareness and under- standing of modern technology.

The best way to teach this precept is by example. Never be too proud to ask for information. Every single person working for your company can teach you something.

Knowing when to ask for help (and being prepared to ask for help) is a sign of strength, not weakness. Knowing whom to ask for help (and knowing what questions to ask) is a sign of wisdom, not ignorance.

ENCOURAGE EMPLOYEES TO MAKE SUGGESTIONS

Nothing causes more stress than seeing a solution to a problem and not being able to get anyone to listen to it.

As a student I once worked in a large laboratory in Switzerland where, every day, hundreds of items were tested on sophisticated electronic equipment.

I was new to the work, the laboratory and the company, but I hadn't been there more than a couple of days when I realised that the accepted way of doing things was unnecessarily time consuming (and therefore expensive). There was, it seemed to me, a much quicker way of doing the testing and getting results of the same quality.

I don't know whether it was my inability to communi- cate in German or the unwillingness of the laboratory staff to listen to a junior employee but I couldn't get my idea considered, let alone accepted.

It was deeply frustrating. After another two weeks I couldn't stand it any longer. I left.

The daft thing is, of course, that although I had suffered some temporary frustration, the company concerned probably lost a lot of money.

What happened to me in Switzerland many years ago probably happens several times every day in British industry.

The man working on the shop floor often sees simple ways to improve working methods that skilled management advisers have been unable to improve even after months or years of study. The office employee who studies a particular problem every day for months on end may eventually produce a neat, cheap solution to an expensive and complex problem. The junior assistant who is innocent and new to everything may see an obvious solution that has evaded everyone else.

So, there are real advantages in encouraging suggestions from everyone in your company.

And I don't just mean by having a suggestions box nailed to the wall in the canteen.

At the very least it should be possible for anyone in the company to make an oral or written suggestion for improvements to a departmental head. Then, if the suggestion is accepted, he should be praised and thanked formally. If for some reason the suggestion is not practicable then the employee should be told why his suggestion won't work. At best the company should organise a proper incentive scheme whereby employees get commercial fees for practical and useful suggestions.

All this benefits the company twice.

First, there are the purely practical benefits of having a work force which contributes to the company's efficiency and productivity.

Secondly, and infinitely more important, employees are positively encouraged to take an active interest in their company. Potential frustrations are eased and stresses strangled at birth.

You may find this difficult to believe, but employees commonly become far more loyal to their company when they think they have played a part in helping in its success. When I was a lad I worked in the summer holidays in a factory making switchgear. One of the men in the shop where plastic mouldings were prepared was given the job of looking after me on my first morning. I'll never forget the pride on his face and in his voice when he showed me a gadget he himself had designed to help chip mouldings clean of extraneous plastic. I'm convinced it was his pride that led to his loyalty. And you can't buy real loyalty.

The best suggestions sometimes come from the most unlikely sources.

MAKE SURE YOUR COMPANY SHOWS THAT IT CARES

I asked a man I know who has a responsible management post in banking what his company does to show its employees that it really cares.

The only thing he could think of was that it provided free health insurance.

He honestly seemed to think that this made his company one of the great caring monoliths of the twentieth century.

I didn't know whether to laugh or to cry.

Buying health insurance cover for employees may seem like a cheap way to show compassion and care. But it isn't particularly cheap and it isn't particularly effective.

The fact is that in most countries today the State provides an excellent service for people who know how to use it properly. If you know where to go,. you don't have to wait for an operation. If you know the ropes you can get a private bed for a modest cost.

And what is true of health care is also true of housing, social services, schooling and so on. The problem is not that the facilities aren't there but that for many people they are difficult to reach: fighting through bureaucracy requires skill, knowledge, determination and a little power.

Those fighting strengths are denied the average employee.

Here is the alternative 'caring solution' that I suggested to the man at the bank.

Instead of simply buying health insurance, spend the money on hiring a company 'social interpreter'.

Put him (or her) in an office and give him the job of helping employees get the best out of the State and local authority administrators. A sort of Company Advice Bureau. The 'social interpreter' could provide help for both employees and their immediate families.

The company would benefit in a number of ways. Your employees would get the best possible service from the many available statutory facilities; employees would know that the company cared and was prepared to fight for them; they would spend less time worrying and they would save time too. The man waiting for a hernia operation would be able to beat the waiting list and get back to work six months sooner. The woman looking after her aged mother would be able to get back to work if a place in an old people's home could be sorted out quicker. The woman looking for a creche for her three year old would be able to accept more responsibility.

A halfway competent adviser could easily look after a company population of 1,000.

Work out the sums. It makes excellent financial sense. The company would make a real cash profit on the project. And, most important of all, employees would see that their company really cared about them.

A company that cares is a company that profits.

ENCOURAGE SENSIBLE EXERCISE HABITS

Kenneth B, a production manager at a car component factory, thought he was as fit as any man of his age. He went running twice a week and played squash every Sunday morning. He believed that by exercising regularly he was helping himself to stay healthy and control the effects of stress on his life.

He had a heart attack and died two weeks after his fortieth birthday.

Kenneth's mistake had been in the type of exercise he chose.

The first problem was that he didn't exercise regularly enough. To be useful and healthy, exercise needs to be regular. It should be gentle and thorough rather than aggressive and exhausting.

The second problem was that he was as competitive when exercising as he was when working. He constantly pushed himself to run faster and faster. He hated to lose a squash match. His exercise rituals didn't detract from the amount of stress in his life: they added to it.

The truth is that simple types of exercise — walking, dancing, swimming and cycling for example — are the best and most natural forms of exercise anyone can take. Marathon running and squash are more dangerous than contact sports such as boxing.

Tough, aggressive, competitive exercise *increases* — rather than reduces — stress levels.

PERSONALISE THE ENVIRONMENT

Walk around your company and look at the notices and posters that are stuck up.

You'll learn a good deal about just how your company perceives its employees — and how your employees feel about the company.

If the only notices are fire drill regulations, safety posters and notices about the annual Christmas dinner then you've got problems.

For the cost of a few notice boards and pin boards you can buy allegiance!

Encourage employees to use the notice boards to advertise goods for sale, part-time skills and unwanted time-sharing accommodation. Let their children advertise services as baby sitters, car washers, lawn cutters etc.

And give someone in each department the job of preparing a weekly newsletter detailing births, marriages, holidays, personal achievements and so on.

For the price of a few square yards of cork and a few hundred drawing pins the company will benefit in a number of ways: company loyalty will be improved, companionship will be improved and stress levels will go down.

The type of notices on your walls says a lot about your company.

MAKE SURE EMPLOYEES KNOW HOW TO RELAX

Ask the average employee how he relaxes and he'll probably say, 'Well, I go home, put my slippers on, sit in front of the fire, have a cold beer in my hand and watch the television.'

It *sounds* like a relaxing way to spend an evening.

But it isn't enough.

The individual who has been under pressure all day will not relax properly simply by settling down in front of the television with a drink in one hand and the remote control operator in the other.

His body may feel relaxed but the chances are that his mind will still be churning over the day's events.

Proper relaxation — of both mind and body — requires some thought and care. Yet relaxation skills really aren't difficult to learn. It will cost very little to teach your employees how to relax properly. But you'll save untold thousands by keeping people healthy and avoiding losses in production.

The individual who learns how to deal with stress by relaxing his mind will benefit in a variety of different ways. He will be stronger, healthier and far less vulnerable to worry and anxiety than the individual who is at the mercy of each day's new stresses and strains.

Consider Roger, for example. For years now he has worked as a television presenter. During that time he has developed a number of stress induced problems. Early in his career he developed a stomach ulcer and that was soon followed by raised blood pressure. He has also suffered from persistent arthritis in his knees. To help him cope with the day–to–day pressures of presenting a live television programme he has regularly used cigarettes and tranquillising drugs.

Eventually, it all got too much for him. His edginess began to shown through and the drugs he needed to help him stay calm reduced his ability to think quickly and clearly. He was told that his contract might not be renewed.

The warning inspired Roger to try to learn how to relax. He chose 'daydreaming' — perhaps the simplest and most effective technique there is.

Every day Roger disappeared for ten minutes at a time and hid himself in his dressing room. There he would lock the door, put ear plugs in and settle himself down in a comfortable easy chair. He would deliberately try to imagine that he was sunning himself on a beach somewhere. Underneath the room's most powerful lamp, and with his eyes closed, he would imagine that the heat he could feel from the lamp was being produced by the sun's rays.

He would imagine that he was lying on a warm, sunny beach.

It was a midsummer day and yet the beach was quite deserted. In the distance to his right and left there were one or two families scattered around and he could just hear the faint sound of children playing. In front of him the waves were breaking gently on the soft sand and behind him a slight breeze rustled through the long grasses of the sand dunes. High above he could hear the seagulls calling to one another as they circled overhead. They and the far off children were the only sounds that disturbed the peace and tranquillity of that scene.

The most insistent sensation was that of warmth. The sand beneath him was warm and the sun was warm on his skin.

He 'knew' that if he opened his eyes he would be startled by the brightness of the sun. And so he stayed still; enjoying the silence, the peace and the warmth.

After ten minutes of mental relaxation he would emerge from his dressing room relaxed and ready to continue.

After doing this for a couple of weeks Roger found that he didn't need to lock himself in his dressing room in order to 'escape' from the pressures that were surrounding him in the studio. He needed only to close his eyes and let his mind do the rest. He even found that he could relax in the studio.

Once the daydreaming technique has been mastered it guarantees an escape from pressure and stress and an immunity to stress induced disease.

You don't have to use the same daydream that Roger used, of course. You can use just about any scene you like.

Each individual can build up a library of his (or her) very own, private daydreams. He can store a valuable collection of happy memories. Some can be real, some may be memories taken from films or television programmes. Others may be based on scenes that have been encountered in favourite books.

Relaxation — like playing golf or dancing — is a skill that needs to be learnt. But once learnt it is a skill that will last for ever.

ALWAYS KEEP COMMUNICATION LINES OPEN

Communications are crucial — they are the lifeblood of any company.

A good executive will be available to the people working for him. He doesn't have to keep an ever open door but he should be available for *some* time every day.

Highly successful American businessman T. Boone Pickens Jr. says, 'My people know that they can talk to me, no matter how busy I am. So, when it's time to make a decision I'm ready, with no need for lengthy presentation. Communication means no surprises. I hate surprises.'

Try to keep your lines of communication as simple and informal as possible.

Remember that the memo is one of the most dangerous and stress inducing of all industrial weapons.

Many managers fire off memos at a ridiculous rate.

This habit can be counterproductive — and extremely destructive.

First, you have to remember what the function of the company is. If the company makes money out of memos then that's fine. Keep on with the memos. But in most companies memos cost a good deal of money in terms of the time spent in their preparation, execution, transmisson and receipt. Before firing off another memo you should ask yourself whether or not it is really necessary.

Second, memos can be dangerous because of the anxieties they produce. Ambitious, rising executives frequently spend hours trying to read between the lines of J.G.'s latest memo. They look for all sorts of hidden messages and innuendoes. Their paranoia and corporate fear is easily fed by a regular diet of company memos.

Try to keep your lines of communication as simple as possible. Writing things down is the best way to keep records but talking is the natural way to do business — and talking generates ideas.

Remember that the best and most accurate way to communicate is to talk to someone. Either pick up the telephone and make a call or, even better, wander down the corridor and see if the person you want to reach can spare a moment. He probably can if he doesn't have too many memos to read. In a face to face conversation it is much easier to exchange information without starting a whole new batch of stress inducing rumours.

Finally, remember that if your lines of communication remain open then potential problems can usually be solved before they grow too large. In the long run you'll cut down the amount of stress that both you and those who work for and with you have to suffer.

One conversation is worth a thousand memos.

PUT PURPOSE INTO PEOPLE'S LIVES

Once upon a time there were two bricklayers. They both did exactly the same work for the same local builder.

The first bricklayer found his work extremely tedious. 'All I do every day is lay one brick on top of another,' he complained. 'I get to work at 8.30 and lay bricks until it is time for lunch. Then after lunch I lay bricks until it is time to go home. My only moment of satisfaction is when I pick up my wage packet on a Friday afternoon.'

He was away from work at least three days a month — usually complaining of aching muscles, a vague headache or a touch of backache. His real complaint, however, was a complete lack of enthusiasm for his work. Whenever there was an excuse to join an industrial dispute he would be the first man to lay down his trowel in the interests of industrial disharmony.

The second bricklayer enjoyed his work. 'I build houses,' he said proudly. 'Every day I think of the people who will occupy the house I am building. I think of their joy when they first see their new home. I think of the family that will grow up in it. I think of the generations who will decorate it and regard it as 'home'. I don't think of myself as building a wall or even a house. I'm building someone a home.'

This bricklayer was hardly ever away from work. He certainly never missed Monday mornings as some of his colleagues were wont to do.

If you can explain to each employee exactly what they are doing — and who will benefit — then you will give their lives added purpose and meaning.

Does everyone in your company know exactly what the company produces and who benefits?

CONTROL COMPETITIVENESS

In all companies there is inevitably a good deal of competition between employees looking for promotion.

To a certain extent competition is healthy.

But it can easily get out of hand. Employees can suffer if they feel that they are failing in an exceptionally competitive atmosphere.

In particular, you need to watch out for the 'apple for the teacher' syndrome in which an ambitious employee ingratiates himself with a manager to further his own career.

It can be very flattering for someone in a management post to acquire a young acolyte. But this sort of unfair competition can easily annoy and alienate other employees. Once it is felt that employees are being favoured for personal reasons rather than professional ones the quality of work done will probably diminish.

All may be fair in love and war, but that's not true of business.

SHOW PEOPLE THAT YOU ARE INTERESTED IN THEM

Really good salesmen carry a small card index around with them. They would rather go out into the field without a suit, a case of samples and a pack of visiting cards than without their card index.

When they arrive at a client's they will stop for a moment and flick through the card index before picking out the relevant entry. Then they will refresh their memories about the client.

They'll rediscover that he has a wife and three children: Tony, Michael and Penelope. They'll find the ages of the children, the client's birthday and his wedding anniversary date. They'll see that he likes powerboat racing and water skiing and that he spends two weeks every year in the Canary Islands. They'll be reminded of the type of jokes he prefers, his religion and his political preferences. They'll see instantly what type of food he likes best and the type of drink he prefers.

Only when they have armed themselves with all this information will they go in to see their client. They won't make overt use of any of this information, of course. But they will use it to enable them to make the client feel loved and important.

At the end of the call the client will feel good. He will be pleased that the salesman 'remembered' his name and the names of his children. He will be impressed when the salesman 'remembers' that he goes to the Canary Islands every year. He will feel flattered and important. Deep down in his heart he'll probably know that the information all comes from a card index. But it won't matter. He'll like the salesman and so he'll like the product he's selling.

What amazes me is that although this system works very well for salesmen, managers and executives hardly ever use it to improve their relationships with their employees.

If you let your employees know that you are interested in them then they will be more loyal, they will work harder and they will be more enthusiastic about working for you and the company.

BANISH AMBIGUITY

Clarity in communication is vital in any company.

Sometimes, misunderstandings and confusion occur by accident. A comma in the wrong place can change the whole meaning of a sentence and can result in a complete and perhaps unwanted change of company policy.

Sometimes misunderstandings and confusion occur because someone is covering his rear.

Don't let people get away with memos that can be read in two quite different ways or with reports that mean different things to different people.

Ambiguity — whether deliberate or accidental — leads to pressure, stress, errors and expensive mistakes.

AVOID CONFLICTING RULES AND REGULATIONS

It is extremely stressful to be told one thing by one boss and something quite different by another.

Not only does this sort of confusion lead to a lack of respect and a lack of efficiency — it also leads to endless uncertainties and crippling anxieties.

In a large organisation, conflicting regulations and rules can easily produce problems. The easiest way to avoid this is to keep the number of regulations and rules to an absolute minimum.

Rules are for schoolchildren anyway.

Keep an eye out for conflicting advice. Make sure that company policies are clear and unequivocal.

CRITICISE — BUT WITH CARE AND THOUGHT

From time to time everyone needs criticism. But the way in which you offer criticism will affect the criticised individual's response both in the short and long term.

There are three important things to remember.

First, try whenever possible to offer constructive criticism. Don't just condemn a man for not doing something. Explain to him how he could have done what you wanted him to do.

Second, don't criticise in public. That isn't criticism — it's humiliation.

Third, when exposing someone's bad points try to balance your criticism with a little praise. Generally speaking people prefer praise to criticism. When an individual is praised he feels a warm glow inside. He feels wanted and respected. And he wants to please the person who has done the praising so that he'll get even more praise in the future. He will, therefore, respond to your criticisms more speedily.

The carrot and the stick work together well.

USE ENCOURAGEMENT TO STRENGTHEN THE WEAK

In any company there will be excellent employees who lack self confidence and who are, at times, vulnerable and inadequate. Employees of this type are often exceptionally hard working, unusually loyal and particularly creative.

If you recognise that a valued employee is showing

signs of a lack of self confidence (or inadequacy) then try to boost his self assurance by reminding him whenever possible of his virtues and his strengths.

Encouragement costs nothing but pays huge dividends.

IT'S THE LITTLE THINGS THAT COUNT

Grown–ups often behave like children. But they hide their feelings better. And when they get upset they get upset for longer.

Tony worked for a large international oil company. He had a responsible well paid job. He was happy. And then he was promoted to an even more responsible, even better paid job. You'd have thought he would have been thrilled. But he wasn't.

When he came to see me he couldn't sleep and was having genuine panic attacks.

I asked him if he thought the work was too much for him. He said it wasn't.

I asked him if he had money problems. He said he hadn't.

I asked him if he had problems at home. He said he hadn't.

I asked him if he had troubles with people at work. He said he hadn't.

I gave up. I pleaded with him to tell me what was the matter.

In the end he told me that all the other senior departmental managers had 2.1 litre cars but he still had only a 1.6 litre. He said he thought that might mean his promotion was only temporary.

I asked him if he had thought to ask anyone why he

hadn't been offered a new car. He said he hadn't. I suggested he had a word with the man in charge of the motor pool.

Tony telephoned me the next morning with a smile in his voice. He told me the man in charge of the motor pool had confirmed that a new 2.1 litre car was on order but that they were having to wait a little longer than usual for the car to come through..

This may sound like a trivial anecdote. But, believe me, it isn't. Status symbols are terribly important. They are an outward sign of success. And it is desperately important that care is taken to make sure that symbols always match.

It isn't just getting the key to the executive washroom that is important. The size of the keyring is important too.

REMEMBER THE LOSER

If you are making a new appointment then think about the people who aren't going to get the new job — the ones who are being passed over. Call them into your office before the appointment is made public and break the news gently.

It isn't easy for you but it will make things a lot easier for them and you may retain the loyalty and enthusiasm of someone who could easily have become unhappy and dissatisfied.

Remember, the man you overlook today may be your boss tomorrow.

LEARN TO ANTICIPATE PROBLEMS

Being able to deal with problems effectively and quickly is important. But the executive who can spot problems before they develop — and deal with them before they become costly and disruptive — is of far more value to the company.

In order to spot problems at an early stage you need to understand the people who work for your company. You need to know what makes them tick. You need to know their individual strengths, weaknesses, fears, ambitions and hopes. You need to know their relationships and their loyalties.

And you need to know how they are likely to react in specific circumstances.

So, for example, if you have a good idea how Joe will respond when you make Clive foreman over his head then you may well be able to defuse a potentially explosive situation by talking to Joe in advance. If you know what his objections are likely to be then your job will be a lot easier. Of course, you may not be able to prevent Joe from leaving or causing trouble. But at least you will be able to prepare for it.

Once you are prepared for a problem, the problem becomes less significant.

MAKE THE MOST OF PEOPLE'S SKILLS

Judith worked for a large insurance company as a senior secretary. But she was bored. She did her job well enough but it wasn't much of a challenge. Her real love was writing. In her spare time she wrote a column every week for the local newspaper. They didn't pay her very much but she enjoyed it.

Gradually, as the months went by, she started to spend more and more time writing and less and less time being secretary. Her boss caught her writing articles in his time. But he didn't want to lose her. Even on half power she was worth her money.

He had a brainwave. For some time he had been thinking of introducing a small, quarterly company newspaper for members of staff, shareholders and some of the company's bigger customers. He'd originally planned to bring in a part time editor from outside. But then he had the idea of offering the job to Judith.

She was thrilled. She put her heart and soul into her new job. And the newspaper was a tremendous success.

Some people would have sacked her. Others would have merely put up with an inefficient, bored secretary. Judith's boss managed to get the best of both worlds. He retained an excellent secretary. And found a way to use her talents to the company's best advantage. Judith had an outlet for her creative talents. Her life had purpose. Everyone benefited, and everyone was happy.

A fancy peg is wasted in a square hole.

REMEMBER THAT COLONIALISM DOESN'T WORK

American executives commonly start the day with a breakfast meeting held in a hotel dining room.

Japanese executives start the day performing exercises alongside shop floor workers.

German executives start work the minute they arrive at their offices.

English executives start work with a cup of tea, a few moments idle gossip and a flick through the morning mail.

Every nation has its own habits, patterns and customs. There is an American way of doing things, a Japanese way of doing things, a French way of doing things, a German way of doing things and an English way of doing things.

The big mistake is to assume that one way is right and all the other ways are wrong.

The American executive who sweeps into an English factory and expects everyone to start doing things the way people do things back home in Idaho is creating a host of problems for himself.

Amusement and surprise will quickly develop into resentment. Employees who feel uncomfortable with and frightened by the American way will lose enthusiasm.

The Japanese executive who opens a factory in Scotland and expects everyone to start the day with exercises and the company song will annoy and embarrass his employees.

The executive in a multi-national company should always try to respect local customs and attitudes and to introduce foreign thinking only when it can clearly be shown to be of value.

When in Rome do as the Romans do. When in Tokyo do as the Japanese do. And when in Manchester do as the English do.

ALLOW EMPLOYEES TO SHOW THEIR ANGER

Anger is one of the commonest, most fundamental and most damaging of human emotions. It can be produced by disappointment, frustration or a real or apparent injustice. It is inspired by indifference, thoughtlessness, officiousness and a host of annoying situations.

Whatever causes it, anger can be physically, mentally, socially and economically damaging. Stored, suppressed anger produces high blood pressure, stomach ulceration, heart disease and all the other symptoms of stress induced disease.

Anger is so often linked to pain and discomfort that we describe red, painful burns and wounds as 'angry' looking.

In order to reduce the damaging effects of anger you should try to encourage your employees to express their anger.

There are several ways in which employees can express their anger and release the tension that may otherwise accumulate inside them and cause problems.

First, try to ensure that there are pathways for protest within any organisation.

Many office or shop floor employees will feel uncomfortable about taking their complaints to their immediate superiors. Indeed, their complaints may be about their immediate superiors. If there is no outlet for their anger then frustration will simmer away until it explodes and produces genuine physical damage.

Try to make sure that every single employee in your organisation can make his complaints known to a neutral observer. If necessary appoint a Company Ombudsman to listen to complaints and absorb anger as it is released.

Secondly, provide some facilities where employees can get rid of their accumulated tensions and anger. Hitting a squash ball or tennis ball, or kicking a football around, can all help employees get rid of their aggression. Alternatively, install a gymnasium where employees can try hitting the stuffing out of a company punch-bag.

Finally, remember that anger is a perfectly natural and reasonably healthy response to stressful circumstances. Everyone gets angry from time to time and suppressing anger — or refusing to acknowledge its existence — can be dangerous.

Remember, people only get angry because they care. By showing that you care too, their anger will do less damage.

ENSURE YOUR EMPLOYEES TAKE THEIR HOLIDAYS

Some executives I know take pride in the fact that they haven't had a holiday for years. Many of those executives expect their employees to forgo their holidays too.

Of course, if you really *want* to have a heart attack, burn out and die early then this sort of blind dedication is understandable.

But if you want to work well, remain efficient and creative and retain your health, then holidays are important. And if you want to keep your employees healthy and efficient then it is important that they too take their holidays regularly.

People who work incessantly, pushing themselves for fifty–two weeks a year, quickly become jaded and tired. They may think that they are still working well but too often they are merely following a long established pattern. All sparkle and enthusiasm disappears.

As a general rule, six months on and two weeks off is an ideal scenario for a healthy lifestyle.

All work and no play makes Jack dull, lacklustre, and inefficient.

REMEMBER THAT 'FAILURE' ISN'T ALWAYS A DIRTY WORD

Some executives I know regard 'failure' as the dirtiest word in the English language.

What they perhaps forget is that the only people who never fail are the people who never take risks. And people who never take risks never achieve anything.

A clever executive will make it clear to those working for him that although he isn't fond of failure he is prepared to accept it — occasionally — as an inevitable part of life. The executive who doesn't make this clear will find that those working for him will waste considerable amounts of time, energy, willpower and money persevering with schemes that they *know* are doomed to failure.

The clever executive will encourage his subordinates to examine their failures carefully. He will insist that every failure be turned into a practical lesson.

The narrow–minded executive will never learn anything from failures because no one close to him will ever admit that there has been a failure.

The clever executive will allow those working for him to admit their mistakes and back away from projects for which there is no longer hope.

The stupid executive who insists that failure is unacceptable will be surrounded by people who are reluctant to take decisions, unwilling to accept responsibility and unable to move forwards for fear of sliding backwards. The subordinates of the executive who cannot accept failure will spend much of their time denying or concealing their errors, or looking for ways to put the blame on others.

The executive whose ego is so fragile that he cannot countenance failure will be surrounded by people who never learn from their mistakes. When an error is made, the resultant fear and trembling will destroy him.

The executive who accepts failure as an inevitable, occasional step on the route to greater success and who is tolerant of those working for him and with him, will cope well with adversity and will suffer less than anyone when a potential disaster occurs.

Risk and failure are inseparable bedfellows. But risk and success are bedfellows too. It stands to reason, therefore, that you can't hope to succeed without accepting the occasional failure.

DON'T FUSS!

Most really successful businessmen confirm that it is vitally important to know how to delegate work to subordinates if you are going to become successful.

Proper delegation — 'hands off management' — means that you will be free to make policy decisions and to keep a close eye on overall management.

Delegating responsibility to subordinates will help them too. Few things are more stressful than being asked to do something and then being constantly subjected to a barrage of questions and reminders.

Before writing a memo or making a telephone call all executives should ask themselves whether their interference is really necessary — or whether they are becoming obsessive fusspots.

Remember that too many rules, too many meetings, and too many reports will cost money, ruin efficiency and destroy the morale of the people who should be doing the work.

Sending a stream of memos and reminders to a downline manager is like reminding a 40 year old to put on a clean vest and pick up a fresh handkerchief.

MASTER THE ART OF THE REPRIMAND

No one likes to be told off.

If you do it the wrong way then the person on the uncomfortable end of the reprimand will hate you for life. Your working relationship will be in ruins and the chances are that instead of solving a problem you will have created a crisis.

If you do it the right way the person getting the reprimand will feel grateful, your relationship will be strengthened and the problem will be unlikely to arise again.

So, what is the wrong way and what is the right way?

First, it is wrong to tell someone off in front of witnesses. If you do, they will hate you, and the witnesses to the reprimand will feel uncomfortable.

Arrange to take the employee somewhere private where you can talk without being overheard. If you're sacking someone for gross misconduct then you can make the whole thing as public as you like. But if you want the offender to carry on working for you and the company then make the reprimand a personal affair.

Second, don't bluster in without knowing what you are going to say.

If you do you're quite likely to end up saying something

you regret. You may lose an otherwise good employee. You may talk yourself into an uncomfortable or embarrassing corner.

Plan your reprimand beforehand. Consider exactly what the problem is, define the possible complications and decide on a range of suitable punishments.

Third, don't simply shout and scream.

You will do far more good if you explain why a reprimand is necessary.

Telling someone off is one of the most difficult things an executive has to do. It is essential to do it well.

Always think before you shout.

GOOD PLANNING CAN HELP TO DEFUSE DEADLINES

In a recent survey conducted by a large multi-national brewery, employees confessed that they considered urgent deadlines to be the overwhelming cause of the stress in their lives.

There isn't anything very surprising about that, of course. Working against the clock is always stressful. Having to battle to beat deadlines adds a good deal of pressure to anyone's life.

But although deadlines are inevitable in most industries they really should not be a major source of daily stress. After all, most of the time, deadlines are defined weeks or even months in advance.

The problems really arise when deadlines are forgotten or ignored until the last minute. The solution, therefore, isn't difficult to see. Executives should do what they can to ensure that proper planning is done on a daily basis in order to ensure that deadlines are not ignored or overlooked.

If you want to take the 'dead' out of deadlines you have to put the 'plan' into planning.

INDEX

INDEX

Also published by Mercury Books

FIT FOR BUSINESS

By Matthew Archer

There is ample evidence that achieving physical fitness not only improves the chances of living longer but also makes people more efficient – mentally as well as physically.

The benefits of physical exercise, sensible eating and adopting a particular lifestyle and attitude can improve the effectiveness of the business executive and provide a defence against stress-related problems.

To achieve this kind of fitness and to maintain it require no great agony. The executive who travels on business, eats working lunches and is subjected to pressure need not adopt the regime of an Olympic athlete or try to live on a diet of muesli and vitamin pills. This book, written by a fit executive, takes the fitness question apart and puts it together again in a practical form which busy executives can use.

ISBN 1 85251 045 5   £10.95 (Hardcover)
ISBN 1 85252 004 3   £6.99 (Paperback, June 1991)